ANIMAL RECORD BREAKERS

THIS IS A CARLTON BOOK

© Carlton Books Limited 2012

Senior Editor: Anna Bowles
Senior Art Editor: Andrew Watson
Design: Tall Tree
Cover Design: Ceri Hurst
Production: Dawn Cameron

Published in 2012 by Carlton Books Limited
An imprint of the Carlton Publishing Group
20 Mortimer Street, London, W1T 3JW

A catalogue record for this book is
available from the British Library.

ISBN: 978 1 78097 205 3
Printed in Dubai

ANIMAL RECORD BREAKERS

STEVE PARKER

CARLTON KiDS

CONTENTS

ANIMAL RECORD BREAKERS

★ ★ ★ ★ ★ ★

ALL KINDS OF ANIMALS

OCEAN-GOING GIANTS

The blue whale is famously the biggest animal. A close second is the fin whale, at 27 metres and 70-plus tonnes. It's also the fastest of the great whales, at 40 kilometres per hour.

GIANT OF THE SWAMPS

The arapaima (or pirarucu) loves South America's swamps. It's probably the world's largest freshwater fish, over 2.5 metres long and weighing 150 kilograms.

Hardly anywhere in the world lacks animals. From the highest mountain to the deepest sea, all kinds of creatures crawl, slither, run, roll, fly and swim their way to record-breaking achievements.

Each kind of animal is suited to a particular type of place. This is known as its habitat – from a little wood to an enormous desert, a small pond to a vast ocean. Animal record-breakers thrive in all of these places, and some are so adaptable that they are found in several habitats.

POLAR RULER

Living near the South Pole, emperor penguins are the largest of the penguin family, at 1.2 metres tall. They lay eggs and raise their chicks through the Antarctic winter.

HOME FROM HOME

The prize for the most adaptable animal could go to the red fox – and for the most cunning, too! Few other creatures thrive in more habitats and on more continents.

HIGH-MOUNTAIN HUNTER

The highest-dwelling predator is the snow leopard. With its thick fur and wide 'snowshoe' paws, it stalks prey 6,500 metres up in Central Asian mountains.

LITTLE LAKE-DWELLER

In huge Lake Baikal, Russia, live the smallest true seals, and the only ones to live in fresh water. Baikal seals are just 1.3 metres long and protected from hunters by law.

WOODLAND RARITY

The northern hairy-nosed wombat is one of the rarest creatures on Earth. Only about 140 survive in one tiny patch of gum-tree woodland in Queensland, Australia.

ALONE IN THE DESERT

Asian desert people keep domesticated Bactrian (two-humped) camels for milk, meat, hair and skins. But truly wild Bactrian camels now number fewer than 1,000.

SUMATRAN ORANGUTAN

Our closest animal cousins are other great apes – chimps, bonobos, gorillas and orangutans. Sumatran orangs are rare, with less than 7,000 remaining.

THE ANIMAL KINGDOM

To help us understand the natural world, all creatures are grouped together as the Animal Kingdom. This is divided into subgroups, then into smaller groups, and so on.

It's difficult to describe what is an animal, and what is not.
There are usually exceptions:

★ Most animals have a brain, but jellyfish and starfish do not.

★ Most animals move about, but barnacles do not.

★ The most general feature of animals is that they take in ready-made food by some means, usually by eating. This sets animals apart from plants, fungi and other kinds of living things.

ANIMALS WITH BACKBONES

AMPHIBIANS
Begin life as tadpoles
Frogs, toads, salamanders, newts
★ The cane toad is one of the worst introduced species, causing havoc to native wildlife in north-east Australia.

FISH
Most have scales and fins, live in water
Sharks, eels, marlin, herring, trout, carp
★ The wels catfish has the largest mouth of any freshwater fish, able to swallow a swan!

REPTILES
Most have scales, lay eggs
Lizards, snakes, crocodiles, alligators, turtles, tortoises
★ The black mamba is the fastest snake.

BIRDS
Wings and feathers, lay eggs
Ostriches, penguins, eagles, starlings, parrots
★ Condors have the largest wing area of all the birds.

MAMMALS
Fur or hair, young feed on mother's milk
Rats, cats, bats, wolves, monkeys, horses, kangaroos
★ The Javan rhino is the world's rarest big animal, with fewer than 50 left.

ANIMALS WITHOUT BACKBONES

JELLYFISH, CORALS, ANEMONES (CNIDARIANS)

Jelly-like body, stinging tentacles to catch prey
☆ The lion's mane jellyfish is largest, over two metres across and with tentacles 30-plus metres long.

SPONGE (PORIFERA)

No brain, nerves or limbs. They filter sea water for food.

MOLLUSCS (MOLLUSCA)

Flexible body. Many have protective shells
Mussels, clams, snails, slugs, octopus

FLATWORMS (PLATYHELMINTHES)

Flattened flexible body
Tapeworms, flukes

WORMS (ANNELIDS, OTHERS)

Tube-like flexible body
Earthworms, leeches, fanworms
☆ One bootlace worm, or nemertean, was the longest-ever animal – over 50 metres!

STARFISH (ECHINODERMS)

Wheel-like body plan
Starfish, sea urchins, sea-lilies
☆ The crown-of-thorns starfish is one of the largest and the most-armed, with over 20 arms.

ROUNDWORMS (NEMATODES)

Tube-like flexible body, no segments (sections)
Pig roundworms, pinworms, threadworms, eelworms

JOINT-LEGGED ANIMALS (ARTHROPODS)

CENTIPEDES

One pair of legs per body segment
Predators
☆ The giant centipede grows to more than 30 cm!

ARACHNIDS

Eight legs when adult
Spiders, scorpions, mites, ticks

INSECTS

Six legs when adult
Flies, moths, beetles, mantises, crickets
☆ Monarch butterflies migrate farther than any other insects, over 4,000 km.

MILLIPEDES

Two pairs of legs per body segment
Plant-eaters

CRUSTACEANS

Hard outer shell, many pairs of legs
Crabs, shrimps, barnacles, krill, woodlice
☆ The biggest American lobster weighed 20 kg!

HEAVYWEIGHT CHAMPION

BLUE WHALE

The blue whale holds the most records of any creature on Earth. Most massive overall, largest tongue, biggest heart and many other body parts, also loudest noise and greatest appetite.

'Bluey' is not just a record-breaker among living creatures. It's probably the bulkiest, heaviest animal ever to exist - bigger than any dinosaur.

The brain is large, but not as great as the sperm whale's (see page 36).

The tongue weighs up to four tonnes - as heavy as an elephant.

BIGGEST APPETITE

Blue whales feed mainly on shrimp-like krill, each smaller than your little finger. In midsummer, when eating most, the whale consumes 40 million krill weighing over three tonnes - each day! However at other times of year it may not eat for several weeks.

Blue whales communicate by grunting at volumes of up to 188 decibels - louder than a space rocket taking off!

🐋 SAVED FROM EXTINCTION

There were probably over 250,000 blue whales worldwide before humans started mass killing them about one hundred years ago. An international ban on this whaling from the mid 1960s helped to save the species, which today numbers between 4,000 and 7,000.

Blue whale
Balaenoptera musculus

LENGTH	Up to 30 m
WEIGHT	More than 150 tonnes
RANGE	Worldwide, even to polar regions
DIET	Krill, small fish, similar sea creatures
HABITAT	Open ocean
CONSERVATION STATUS	ENDANGERED

The blue whale is by far the largest animal, at 30 metres long and weighing close to 200 tonnes.

🐋 SEA FILTER

To feed, the whale opens wide and takes in a huge mouthful of water plus food. Then it closes its mouth and uses its tongue and chin to squeeze the water out through brush-like baleen plates. Krill are trapped on these sieve-like filters, licked off and swallowed.

To pump blood around the vast body, the blue whale's heart is the size of a small family car.

BIGGEST FISH

WHALE SHARK

It's not a whale, but it's as big as one. And it's a shark, yet its teeth are too small to harm you. The whale shark is easily the biggest fish in the sea.

Whale sharks are the ocean's gentle giants. Because they are so big, they are unafraid of almost any threat. This includes curious humans in scuba gear who swim alongside.

The complicated pattern of light and dark spots and patches, especially on the back, is unique to each whale shark. It helps with camouflage as it reflects the dappled sunlight coming down from the surface.

The whale shark's tough skin is among the thickest of any creature on Earth – up to 10 centimetres. It protects against bites from hunting sharks such as great whites, and from killer whales.

The mouth is more than 1.5 metres wide. That's enough to swallow a whole human!

LOTS OF BABIES

Some sharks lay eggs, but the whale shark gives birth to babies called pups. More than 300 develop inside the mother, from the world's largest eggs – over 30 centimetres long. It appears that the pups are born over a long time period of weeks or months, and are up to 60 centimetres long.

The shark's huge tail gives it an excellent burst of speed, easily enough to get away from most ships and boats.

SMALLER AND SMALLER

★ For many years the record of smallest fish was held by the Philippines dwarf goby (below). Males grow to about 10 millimetres long, with females slightly longer at 13-14 millimetres.

★ In 2006 an even tinier fish was discovered living in swamps in Sumatra, Indonesia. Known scientifically as Paedocypris progenetica, it is a cousin of carp and goldfish. The males are 9 millimetres long and the females 10 millimetres.

The shark feeds not with its teeth, but with its gills. These have pad-like filters that catch small food as the water comes in through the mouth and then out through the gill slits, five on each side.

Whale shark
Rhincondon typus

LENGTH	More than 12 m
WEIGHT	Up to 20 tonnes
RANGE	Warm seas and oceans worldwide
DIET	Plankton including small creatures such as shrimps, squid, young fish
CONSERVATION STATUS	Vunerable

FASTEST SPRINTER

CHEETAH

No other land creature beats the cheetah for out-and-out speed – or for reaching it fast. This big cat has been timed at more than 110 kilometres per hour. It may even reach 120 kilometres per hour, which exceeds the motorway speed limit in many countries.

ACCELERATION

☆ The cheetah can go from standstill to 60 kilometres per hour in just three strides.

☆ It breaks 100 kilometres per hour in three seconds.

☆ A family saloon car takes around 8 seconds to reach 100 kilometres per hour, though for a top dragster it's just 0.7 seconds.

When sprinting, the cheetah's breathing rate almost triples to nearly three breaths per second, as it sucks copious amounts of air through its extra-large nostrils. Its heart rate more than doubles to four beats per second.

ENDURANCE

The antelope-like pronghorn of North America is famed as the greatest long-distance animal athlete, racing along at more than 65 kilometres per hour for 20 minutes. It could finish a marathon race in just 40 minutes.

The long backbone arches up and then bows down, tilting the shoulders and hips by more than 90 degrees. This allows the long legs to cover more than 7 metres in a single stride.

The cheetah is fully streamlined, with a small head, a slim rangy body, and a long tail. To aid fast turns, the tail flicks to the side to work as an air rudder.

Unlike other cats, the cheetah cannot fully withdraw, or retract, its large claws into its toe sheaths. But the blunt claws provide it with great grip when picking up speed.

Cheetah
Acinonyx jubatus

LENGTH	1.8-2.2 m
WEIGHT	50-60 kg
RANGE	Africa, West Asia
DIET	Animals, from rats to antelopes
SPEED	More than 110 km/h
CONSERVATION STATUS	Vunerable

FASTEST FLIER

PEREGRINE FALCON

The fastest creature on Earth is not actually on the Earth when at full speed. The peregrine falcon reaches its record-breaking 200-plus kilometres per hour in a special hunting dive called a 'stoop'.

The peregrine 'stoops' onto its prey, usually other birds, and strikes them in mid air. Then it quickly turns around and grabs the victim as it tumbles out of the sky.

SUPER-SPEED FEATURES

☆ On the peregrine's nostrils, small bony lumps called tubercles prevent air from rushing in at maximum speed, which could damage the falcon's breathing passages and lungs.

☆ The 'third eyelid' or nictitating membrane, possessed by most birds, is ideal for protecting the eye from rushing air and dust during the dive.

In its 'stoop' the peregrine folds in its wings and tail, and tucks its feet into its body. This gives least air resistance for most speed.

FASTEST ON THE LEVEL

Although the peregrine falcon holds the out-and-out animal speed record when diving, it is probably not the fastest bird in level flight. Among the contenders for this are various kinds of eider duck, zipping along at 100-plus km/h.

Usually the peregrine hits its victim with its tight-closed foot, like a human boxer's knock-out blow with a clenched fist.

LENGTH	Up to 55 cm
WINGSPAN	Up to 1.2 m
WEIGHT	Female 1.2 kg, male 0.9 kg
RANGE	All continents
DIET	Other birds, also sometimes small animals like rabbits, lizards and squirrels
HABITAT	Varied, from mountains to swamps and semi-desert (rarely thick forest)
CONSERVATION STATUS	No concern

The curved talons (claws) punch the prey to stun it, then grasp it with a vice-like grip to carry it away.

The hooked beak is ideal for delivering the final death blow, then tearing up meaty prey into swallow-sized lumps. The falcon usually tries to carry its meal back to its nest or to a favourite feeding perch.

AIRPORT WORKERS

Peregrines, and also other falcons and hawks, are sometimes used near airports. They chase away flocks of birds that can cause a tragedy if they get sucked into aeroplane propellers or jet engines.

SLOWEST SWIMMER

DWARF SEAHORSE

To swish along at high speed, many fish have six or more fins, including a powerful tail. But the seahorse has such a strange body design that only one fin can help with swimming, and that's on its back!

Because of their small size and strange, elongated body shape, seahorses can only swim along very slowly. The dwarf seahorse can only manage about 2-3 centimetres per minute at its fastest!

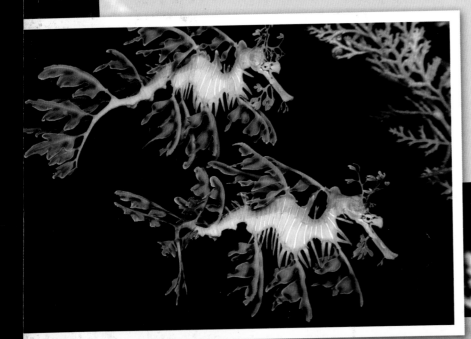

Its skin lacks the usual fish scales and covers a ring-like pattern of bony plates just underneath. This makes the seahorse an uncomfortably crunchy meal for predators.

 CUNNING CAMOUFLAGE

☆ Seahorses have excellent camouflage. Each kind is coloured and shaped to blend with the weeds and rocks around it.

☆ For example, the leafy seadragon (above) has floppy flaps and fringes of skin to match its surroundings.

☆ Another amazing camouflage expert is the sargassum frogfish. Its frilly fins and complicated colours merge perfectly with its seaweedy home.

Unlike most fish, a seahorse 'stands upright' rather than lying underside-down. It has a bent neck so its horse-shaped face points forwards.

LENGTH	5 cm
RANGE	West Atlantic, Caribbean, Gulf of Mexico
DIET	Tiny sea creatures such as shrimps
HABITAT	Warm shallow coastal waters
TOP SPEED	1.5 metres per hour
CONSERVATION STATUS	No special status but its habitat is under threat from pollution, global warming and tourism

The seahorse sucks its tiny prey through its almost-as-tiny mouth, at the end of its long snout.

DOTING DADS

A female seahorse produces eggs, as do most fish. But then she lays them into a pocket-like brood pouch on the male's front. The baby seahorses grow over the course of several weeks, then the father shivers his body to squeeze them out. It looks like he is giving birth!

Seahorse tails are long and curly, adapted for holding onto seaweeds and rocks to avoid being swept away. Once out in a fast current, a seahorse is in big trouble!

FASTEST FISH

SAILFISH

People who fish like to talk about 'the one that got away'. In the case of the sailfish, it can 'get away' in less than a couple of seconds, by racing off faster than a speedboat!

The speediest of all sea creatures, the sailfish can swim as fast as the land speed record-holder, the cheetah, can run – more than 100 kilometres per hour.

The bill slashes and slices to and fro as the sailfish swims through a shoal of prey, to stun and wound victims.

GONE SAILING

At high speed, the sailfish's 'sail' folds down and along its back and upper side. But the sailfish can brake in a couple of seconds and erect its huge, tall fin. Perhaps this frightens the fish it is hunting so they gather into a tight 'baitball', and are easier to catch.

Sailfish are cousins of marlin (right) and swordfish, in the billfish group. They have a similar very long, pointed, super-streamlined snout called the bill.

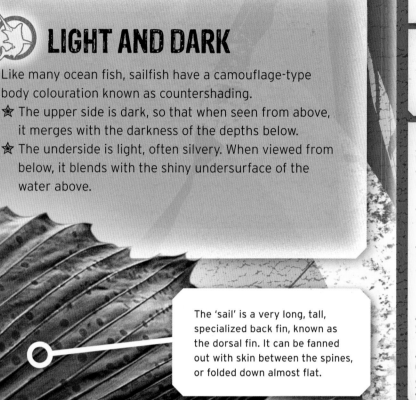

LIGHT AND DARK

Like many ocean fish, sailfish have a camouflage-type body colouration known as countershading.

☆ The upper side is dark, so that when seen from above, it merges with the darkness of the depths below.

☆ The underside is light, often silvery. When viewed from below, it blends with the shiny undersurface of the water above.

Sailfish
Istiophorus platypterus

LENGTH	3-plus metres
WEIGHT	100 kg or more
RANGE	Pacific and Indian Oceans
HABITAT	Warmer open-ocean waters
DIET	Other fish such as mackerel, tuna, sardines, also squid
SPEED	Probably more than 100 km/h
CONSERVATION STATUS	No special status

The 'sail' is a very long, tall, specialized back fin, known as the dorsal fin. It can be fanned out with skin between the spines, or folded down almost flat.

Most swimming power comes from the sailfish's tall, curved, narrow, fairly stiff tail. The fish 'shivers' its body muscles to thrash the tail to and fro many times each second.

The skin of a sailfish can change colour quickly, from dark brown or grey to silver, yellow and pale purple.

SPEEDY SWIMMERS

It's very difficult to measure true fish speeds under the water! Here are some typical estimates for quick bursts:

Seahorse (see page 18) 0.0015 km/h

Sailfish	100-plus km/h
Wahoo	85 km/h
Black marlin	80 km/h
Bluefish tuna	75 km/h
Mako shark	70 km/h

0   70   75   80   85   100+
KM/H

The side fins fold against shallow slots along the body to give better streamlining.

GREATEST TRAVELLER

THE ARCTIC TERN

Why fly almost all the way around the world each year – a distance of more than 70,000 kilometres? The Arctic tern does it just to raise a family.

Each year, Arctic terns fly from the Arctic at the top of the world, to Antarctica at the bottom, and back again. This is the longest of all regular animal journeys, or migrations.

TERN POWER

The tern's immense staying power, or stamina, means that over its lifetime it covers more than 2.4 million kilometres. That's about the same as flying from the Earth to the Moon and back three times!

The red beak, or bill, is well shaped to dip into the water and grab slippery prey, as the tern swoops down to feed.

As for most long-distance fliers, each wing is long and narrow, with a natural up-arching in the middle. This is the best design for staying aloft and using strong winds to glide without flapping.

TERN TRACKING

In recent years, radio tracking devices have become small and light enough to attach to terns, without affecting their flight. Results show that some terns cover more than 80,000 kilometres a year, because they wander and zig-zag to catch the best winds and other conditions.

Arctic tern
Sterna paradisaea

LENGTH	35-37 cm
WINGSPAN	80 cm
WEIGHT	100-110 g
RANGE	Arctic and Far North, Antarctic and Far South
HABITAT	Coastal areas, sea
DIET	Small fish, crabs, shellfish, worms, insects
TOTAL MIGRATION	Up to 80,000 km per year
CONSERVATION STATUS	No special status

The breast muscles, called pectorals, are very large and strong. They pull the wings down with regular power, to keep the bird airborne.

ENDLESS SUMMERS

★ Arctic terns fly north for the Arctic summer, staying up to four months.

★ Near the coast they build nests, lay eggs and raise their chicks.

★ The parents fly at and peck any animal that comes near the nest - including people and even wolves!

★ Then the terns fly south to the Antarctic, just in time for another summer there.

The deeply forked tail gives little air resistance when flying fast. But it can also be fanned out to steer and manoeuvre in high winds.

LONGEST SWIM

GREY WHALE

A swim of more than 10,000 kilometres is just the exercise to build up an appetite. This is what grey whales do every spring, as they head north to their summer feeding areas in the Arctic Ocean.

In autumn, the whales return south to warmer waters, where the mothers have their babies. This annual journey is the longest migration of any sea creature, and by any mammal.

The whale's huge body is heaviest at the end of summer. It has been eating more than one tonne of food daily and storing much of it as fat, to survive the winter when it rarely feeds.

Grey whales prefer shallow water with thick mud on the bottom. They swim along on their side, scooping up enormous mouthfuls of mud and food.

JOURNEY'S END

During winter, grey whales rest in warm sheltered waters, such as Baja California in south-west North America. Here mothers 'calve' or have their babies. The new calf is four metres long and drinks 300 litres of mother's milk each day!

LONG-DISTANCE SHARK

Blue sharks are among the greatest migrating fish. Some cover more than 5,000 kilometres each year in the Atlantic Ocean, and 10,000 in the Pacific.

Brush-like fringes called baleen (whalebone) on the upper jaw filter out the food for swallowing.

The blowholes on the top of the head are the whale's breathing openings – the same as the nostrils in our nose.

WHALE ACROBATICS

Grey whales may be massive, but they are quite agile too! They can...

☆ Breach. The whale picks up speed from the depths and hurls itself out of the water, splashing back with a tremendous crash.

☆ Lobtail. A whale dives, raises its tail flukes in the air and slaps them onto the surface.

☆ Spyhop. With its body vertical, the whale lifts its head above the surface to look around.

Grey whale
Eschrichtius robustus

LENGTH	14 m
WEIGHT	40 tonnes
RANGE	North Pacific and Arctic Oceans
HABITAT	Coastal waters, from nearly tropical to almost freezing
DIET	Seabed animals such as worms, shellfish, shrimps
TOTAL MIGRATION	More than 20,000 km per year
CONSERVATION STATUS	No special status

RECORD-BREAKING REPTILE

SALTWATER CROCODILE

Saltwater crocodiles, or 'salties', are the world's biggest reptiles. A well-fed old male is more than six metres long – as big as a great white shark. He also has possibly the strongest bite on the planet!

Salties are also known as estuarine crocodiles. They do not mind going from fresh water to the salty water of river mouths (estuaries) and the sea.

The nostrils, eyes and ears are all near the top of the head, so the croc can lie low in the water, like a harmless old log, yet still breathe, see and hear.

SPOT THE DIFFERENCE

How can you tell the difference between crocodiles and alligators?
* ☆ Crocs have a long, low head and V-shaped snout.
* ☆ Alligators have a wider, blunter head and U-shaped snout.
* ☆ An alligator's teeth are mostly hidden when its mouth is closed.
* ☆ A croc's lower teeth, especially the fourth one back, often stick outside the upper jaw when the mouth closes.

Through its life, a croc can have more than 3,000 teeth! Each tooth grows for a year or two. Then it breaks off or falls out and a new one grows in its place.

BIG AND SMALL

☆ There are about 23 different kinds of crocodiles and alligators.

☆ Just as long as the saltwater crocodile is the gharial of Southern Asia (left). It can reach more than six metres but it's much slimmer, so it weighs less than 300 kilograms.

☆ Smallest is Cuvier's dwarf caiman. At just 1.3 metres long, it would make a small snack for a big 'saltie'! Luckily for the caiman it lives far away, in South America

The croc's body is covered with bony plates called scutes, which are in turn covered by thick scales. Not many animals can bite through such tough armour.

DANGEROUS DIET

Saltwater crocs are feared as man-eaters. They probably kill hundreds of people each year across South East Asia. Often they lurk unseen in the water, then rear up and knock over boats to grab the people.

On land, crocs like the saltie have a 'high walk', holding the legs almost underneath the body. They can gallop like this at 20 kilometres per hour – maybe faster than you!

Saltwater crocodile
Crocodylus porosus

LENGTH	6 m
WEIGHT	1 tonne
RANGE	South-East Asia, Australia
HABITAT	Rivers, lakes, swamps, shallow sea coasts
DIET	Any animals, from fish and rats to elephants and buffalo
CONSERVATION STATUS	No special status

LARGEST LIZARD

KOMODO DRAGON

Dragons are supposedly huge scaly beasts with sharp teeth and claws, a long tail, wings and the ability to breathe fire.

The Komodo dragon – the world's biggest lizard – manages all this except for the wings and fiery breath.

About 60 jagged-edged teeth, up to 2.5 cm long, give the lizard a ferocious, ripping bite.

The long yellow tongue 'smells' the air to find the dragon's favourite food of dead, rotting animal bodies, or carcasses.

VENOMOUS BITE

Several large monitor lizards, including the Komodo dragon, have venom glands. But it's not clear how strong the venom is. Much more venomous for its size is the Mexican beaded lizard (above) whose bite can easily kill a rat.

Komodo dragons change colour as they grow. Juveniles are green with yellow and black stripes, while adults are brown, grey or red.

Komodo dragon
Varanus komodoensis

LENGTH	3 m
WEIGHT	70 kg
RANGE	A few islands in Indonesia, South East Asia
HABITAT	Open forest, scrub, grassland
DIET	Any animals, from birds and mice to goats, deer and buffalo
CONSERVATION STATUS	Vulnerable

DRAGONS IN DANGER

Komodo dragons take their name from one of the main islands where they live, Komodo in South East Asia. They are rare, with probably fewer than 5,000 in the wild. Most live in protected wildlife parks.

The great claws are curved, sharp and strong. The lizard uses them to climb and to rip open large meals.

HORRIBLE HABITS

A Komodo dragon's mouth is a horrible place!
☆ As well as the teeth, it has lots of dripping saliva (spit).
☆ This is full of harmful bacteria and other germs, which get into the bite wounds of victims.
☆ The dragon also has venom glands (like a snake's).
☆ So any living victim, when bitten, soon dies of shock, blood loss, infection and venom effects.

HIGH-RISE HOME

THE YAK

If you lived in the icy air of the world's tallest mountains, you would need a very warm coat, and a body adapted to getting oxygen from the thin air. The yak has these features, and many more.

Yak are a type of cow suited to the highest homes in the world – the scrub and grasslands of the high Himalayan slopes. Wild yak are rare, while tamed or domestic yak are kept by local people.

The yak's long outer coat has hairs up to one metre long, for protection against wind, rain and snow. Beneath is a thick, soft, woolly undercoat for warmth.

LIKING THE HIGH LIFE

★ Bumblebees have been seen on Mount Everest at more than 5,600 metres.

★ The crow-like bird known as the alpine chough (right) makes its nest and raises its chicks at heights of more than 6,000 metres.

★ Snow leopards have been seen at 6,700 metres in summer, because their prey, such as wild mountain sheep and goats, lives up there too.

Snow Leopard

Chough

Bumblebee

Yak
Bos grunniens

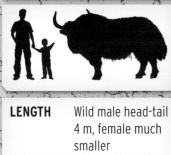

LENGTH	Wild male head-tail 4 m, female much smaller
WEIGHT	Wild male up to 1 tonne
RANGE	Central Asia, including Himalaya Mountains
HABITAT	High-altitude grassland, shrubland and scrub
DIET	Grasses, mosses and similar plants
CONSERVATION STATUS	Wild yak are classed as Vulnerable

YAK HERDING

Domestic yak are about half the weight of wild yak. They provide almost everything for their yak-herders – milk, meat, wool and hair, and horns, hooves and bones to carve into tools and utensils. Yak also carry heavy loads, pull ploughs and even have fun racing!

The shoulder hump stores fat, as a reserve of energy when food is short.

A male yak's horns can grow to one metre long. They are useful for fighting enemies and other males at breeding time. Females have smaller horns.

Yak have huge lungs for breathing in lots of air, and a strong heart to pump blood, which carries life-giving oxygen around the body.

HERDS

Both wild and domestic yak are sociable animals. They like to form herds with others of their kind. Large herds contain cows (females) and calves (young), with perhaps a few bulls (males). Most other males live on their own or in very small 'bachelor' herds.

BIGGEST BIRD

OSTRICH

Taller and heavier than a person, the ostrich is a multi-record-holder. It's the tallest, heaviest and fastest-running of all living birds (although not the biggest-ever bird).

The ostrich also lays the biggest eggs of any creature. And it probably has the widest diet too. It pecks up and gulps down almost any food, plant or animal, from hard nuts to juicy fruits, plus soft worms, scaly snakes, and even animal droppings.

ALL-TIME BIRD RECORDS

☆ Tallest – Giant moa, 3.5 m. It lived in New Zealand until the 1400s.

☆ Heaviest – Giant elephant bird, 400 kg. This massive Madagascan non-flier died out about 500 years ago.

☆ Biggest flier – Giant teratorn, wingspan 7 m and weight 70 kg. A type of vulture, it lived in South America around 6 million years ago.

☆ Biggest egg – Giant elephant bird (see above), 33 cm long, more than 300 times the volume of a hen's egg.

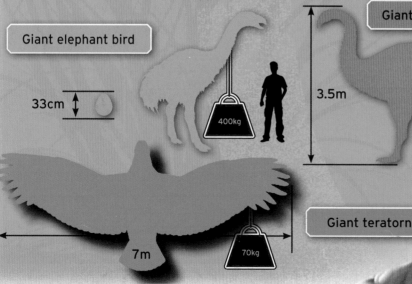

Giant elephant bird

33cm

400kg

Giant moa

3.5m

Giant teratorn

7m

70kg

Each massive foot has two toes tipped with powerful claws. These are fearsome weapons. An ostrich can rip open an enemy with one powerful kick.

At five centimetres across, the eyes are bigger than any other land creature's. They are ideal for peering from their great height across the open woods, grassland, dry scrub and desert of this bird's habitat.

STONE-EATERS

Ostriches swallow small pebbles into their stomach-like gizzard, to help grind up tough food. A single ostrich can carry 2 kg of these stomach-stones or gastroliths around in its body!

The ostrich's wings are useless for flight. But they are more than two metres across when stretched out, and their fluffy feathers make an excellent sunshade to keep the eggs or chicks cool in the nest.

AMAZING EGGS

The hen (female) ostrich lays eggs that are 15-16 cm long and 1.5 kg in weight. Each egg has a volume 25-30 times more than an average hen's egg. But compared to the size of the mother, it's one of the smallest, at 1/70 of her weight. Biggest in this respect is the kiwi's egg, which is 1/4 of the mother's weight.

No bird has longer legs than the ostrich, more than one metre from hip to foot. They allow it to race along with three-metre strides.

SMALLEST BIRD

BEE HUMMINGBIRD

It's as small as a bee, yet it does not buzz – it hums! The bee hummingbird is the world's tiniest bird. It flaps its wings so fast that they look like a blur to our eyes and make a humming sound for our ears.

The long beak or bill probes deep into flowers to sip their sweet, juicy, energy-rich nectar.

The male has a bright red-pink throat and chin, which the female lacks. He is also slightly smaller than her.

FLOWER FEAST

Hummingbirds poke their long, thin bills into flowers, to lick out the thick, sugary fluid called nectar. The tongue is even longer than the bill and sticks out of its end. The bee hummingbird also pecks up small bugs such as ants, caterpillars and spiders. At night time, bats hover-feed in the same way.

HOVER-BIRDS

Hummingbirds hover in mid air, and even fly backwards, by flapping their wings really fast. The wing's front or leading edge faces mainly upwards, as the rear or trailing edge twists forwards and then backwards, with the wingtip tracing out a figure-8 shape.

HUNGRY HOVERERS

There are more than 320 different kinds of hummingbird. They live in warm parts of the Americas. To power their active, high-speed lives, they eat their own weight in nectar and other foods every day (below).

The shoulder joint twists through 180 degrees as the wings flap while hovering.

The powerful wing-beating muscles in the chest make up one-third of the bird's total weight!

The brilliantly coloured feathers glow in the sun. They are iridescent, changing hue as the light falls on them from different directions.

The hummingbird can hardly walk at all. Its tiny feet are used only for perching.

Bee hummingbird
Mellisuga helenae

LENGTH	5-5.5 cm
WEIGHT	1.5-2.5 g
WINGSPAN	3-3.5 cm
WINGBEATS	80 beats per second
HABITAT	Subtropical forests, swamps, gardens
RANGE	The island of Cuba, in the West Indies
DIET	Nectar, small bugs
CONSERVATION STATUS	No special status

BIGGEST BRAIN

SPERM WHALE

The sperm whale is not only the world's most massive predator. It also has the biggest brain on the planet – about six times the size of a human brain.

The sperm whale holds other records too. It dives deeper in the ocean, and stays underwater longer, than any other mammal. Imagine holding your breath for more than one hour!

When the whale surfaces, it puffs out stale air and moisture as a fountain of spray called the 'blow'. This comes out of its blowhole, the single breathing opening on top of its head.

There are no teeth in the upper jaw. The long, thin lower jaw has about 50 teeth which are cone-shaped to grip slippery squid and fish.

BIG HEAD

The yellowish wax in the huge head works as a 'sound lens'. As the whale hunts, it makes clicks in its breathing passages. The wax focuses or concentrates them into a narrow beam that travels out through the water. The whale listens for any echoes that bounce back off nearby objects. This system, called echolocation, is also used by bats.

The suitcase-sized brain is housed in the whale's enormously large head. But most of the head is taken up with a thick, creamy, waxy substance called spermaceti.

TINY BODIES, BIG BRAINS

• Shrews (below) are almost as small as your thumb - yet one-tenth of this little mammal's body is taken up with its brain!

• Among invertebrates (animals without backbones), the octopus has one of the biggest brains for its body size. The brain is a strange shape too - the octopus's gullet (food tube) goes right through the middle!

Sperm whale
Physeter macrocephalus

LENGTH	20 m
WEIGHT	Over 50 tonnes
RANGE	Worldwide
HABITAT	Open ocean, undersea valleys near coasts
DIET	Squid, octopus, fish
BRAIN WEIGHT	8-9 kg
CONSERVATION STATUS	Vulnerable

A row of small ridges or humps along the back are another guide to telling apart sperm whales from other whales.

The huge tail flukes are mostly straight along their rear edge. This helps to identify the sperm whale as it raises its tail to dive.

DEEP DIVER

Sperm whales can hold their breath for well over one hour, and perhaps even two hours. To catch their prey, they dive as deep as 3,000 metres, where the water is very cold and totally dark.

TOOTHED WHALES

There are around 90 kinds of whales, dolphins and porpoises in the world's oceans. Sperm whales are the biggest of the toothed whales, the group that also includes dolphins and porpoises, and who feed by hunting.

SMARTEST THINKER

CHIMPANZEE

After ourselves, who is the world's cleverest creature? It's difficult to measure animal intelligence. But usually the chimpanzee is at or near the top of the list. Which is probably expected, since the chimp is also our closest relative in the animal kingdom.

Chimps are excellent at solving problems, planning ahead and finding answers to tricky situations. They learn fast, remember well, and adapt their behaviour.

This chimp 'fishes' for termites. It chews the end of a stem and pokes it into a termites' nest. The termites think they are being attacked and grab the stem. The chimp pulls it out and licks off the small, juicy snacks!

BRIGHT SPARKS

Dolphins (below) and octopuses are also clever creatures. Octopuses can find food hidden in boxes by recognizing the marks or symbols on the box. Dolphins even make up their own tricks to teach their trainers.

USING TOOLS

Chimps are among the few animals that use objects as tools, and one of the even fewer creatures who make tools by altering natural objects.

★ They use a flat stone as an 'anvil' and a rounded one as a 'hammer', to smash open hard-shelled nuts and fruits.

★ They tear and squash a soft leaf to use as a 'sponge', to soak up water from a hole that they cannot reach with the mouth.

★ They 'fish' for termites with a stem or twig, having stripped the leaves and chewed one end.

SIGN LANGUAGE

Great apes - chimps, gorillas and orangutans - communicate by dozens of natural face expressions, body postures, and sounds. They can also learn the hand gestures of human sign language, and 'talk' to people. For example, a thirsty chimp might make the sign for water or a drink.

Chimps have excellent hearing, partly because they make so many different calls and sounds for each other. This "chimp talk" is another sign of their intelligence.

Chimpanzee
Pan troglodytes

HEIGHT	Up to 1.5 m
WEIGHT	60 kg
RANGE	West and Central Africa
HABITAT	Forest, scrub
DIET	Fruits, seeds, bark, honey, small creatures
CONSERVATION STATUS	Endangered

Chimp hands are similar to our own. They can grip strongly or delicately. However the thumb is not as long or as flexible as our own thumb.

TALLEST ALIVE

GIRAFFE

If you could stand on three other people who were all standing upright, each on the one below, you would have a giraffe eye's view of the world. This long-necked, long-legged plant-eater is the world's highest creature.

Even a baby giraffe is higher than many other creatures, including most adult humans. When it's born, it is almost two metres tall!

TONGUE TWISTER

A giraffe has the longest tongue of any animal - up to 50 centimetres! It is almost black, very muscular, and prehensile, which means it can curl around and grasp leaves and twigs to pull into the mouth.

PATCHED UP

As with human fingerprints, each giraffe has its own individual, unique pattern of patches, spots and lines. This allows giraffes in a herd to recognize each other and be wary of stranger giraffes they do not know.

COUSINS

★ The giraffe's only close relation is the okapi, a rare antelope-like animal that lives in thick forests in West Africa. Its neck is much shorter, and it has striped legs, like a zebra.

★ The antelope called the gerenuk (below) has a very long neck. It can stand on its rear legs to reach more than two metres high.

When the giraffe lowers its head to drink from a pool, special cut-off valves in its neck slow down the blood flow – otherwise the pressure would burst its brain!

A giraffe has a very powerful heart to pump blood at high pressure all the way up to its brain.

The enormous hooves, big as dinner plates, are excellent self-defence weapons. One kick can easily knock over a lion or similar enemy.

Giraffe
Giraffa camelopardalis

HEIGHT	Males up to 6 m
WEIGHT	Males up to 2 tonnes
RANGE	Central, East and Southern Africa
HABITAT	Grassland, open woodland
DIET	Leaves, buds, fruits, bark
CONSERVATION STATUS	No special Staus

SLEEPIEST CRITTER

ARCTIC SQUIRREL

How would you like to go to bed, sleep through the cold and rain of winter, and wake up six months later, in sunny warm springtime? That's what the Arctic ground squirrel does!

When this plant-eater goes into its deep winter sleep, called hibernation, its body temperature falls from about 37 degrees C (the same as yours) to below zero – the lowest for any mammal.

Arctic ground squirrels are true squirrels. But unlike others in this group, they rarely climb trees. That's because there are none in their cold tundra habitat of grasses, mosses and low, ground-hugging shrubs.

BIG SLEEPERS

☆ Only warm-blooded animals can truly hibernate. They include rodents such as marmots and other ground squirrels, dormice (below) and birchmice, hedgehogs, platypus, and some bats.

☆ Bears, raccoons and skunks fall into a deep sleep during cold spells, but it's not as inactive and extreme as true hibernation.

☆ Cold-blooded creatures like frogs, snakes, fish and butterflies also become inactive in cold conditions. This is known as torpor rather than hibernation. One lungfish woke up after being torpid in a lump of mud for six years!

Arctic squirrel
Spermophilus parryii

LENGTH	40 cm
WEIGHT	0.7-0.9 kg
RANGE	Northern North America
DIET	Leaves, seeds, fruits, buds
HABITAT	Cold grasslands, rocks, tundra
LOWEST TEMP	Minus 3 degrees C
CONSERVATION STATUS	No special status

Like rats, mice and other rodents, the squirrel's front teeth never stop growing. They are kept sharp and the right length by nibbling and gnawing.

The tubby body, shorts ears, blunt nose and short legs are all designed to lose as little heat as possible in the often-frozen Arctic.

In autumn the squirrels are busy collecting food to store in their dens, which have a lining of moss, grass stems and animal hairs.

READY FOR BED

Large cheeks allow the squirrels to gather and store seeds and other foods, to carry back to their burrows. They also eat lots and store energy as body fat.

MOST DAINTILY BUILT

MOUSE DEER

The mouse deer is not the size of a real mouse. But it's still little bigger than a rabbit, with big black eyes, pert ears and pencil-thin legs. So cute!

Mouse deer are also called chevrotains, and there are about 10 different kinds. They are close cousins of true deer, and the smallest of all hoofed animals, or ungulates.

 ## GIANT COUSIN

The biggest type of true deer is the moose of North America, also found in Northern Europe where it is called the elk. This giant stands two metres at the shoulder and weighs 600 kilograms - 300 times as heavy as the mouse deer.

The mouse deer's bulging eyes see well in the gloom of the tropical rainforest.

Males have long upper canine teeth that may stick out of the mouth as tiny tusks.

Lesser mouse deer
Tragulus kanchil

LENGTH	Head-tail 45 cm
HEIGHT	30 cm at the shoulder
WEIGHT	2-2.5 kg
RANGE	South East Asia
DIET	Leaves, other plant parts
HABITAT	Woods, forest
CONSERVATION STATUS	No special status

TINY COUSIN

Another very small hoofed mammal is the royal antelope of Africa. It's about the same height and length as the mouse-deer but slightly heavier in build, weighing three to four kilograms.

The short tail wags fast when the deer is worried or scared.

Mouse-deer tiptoe carefully among the leaves of the forest floor on tiny hooves the size of your little finger's nails.

CAMERA-SHY

Mouse deer are not only small, they are also very secretive, shy and wary. And unlike true deer, who are mostly herd creatures, mouse deer tend to live alone or in pairs. So it's very difficult to find them in thick forest. Most photographs are taken by automatic cameras set off by the mouse deer's movements.

LARGEST ON LAND

AFRICAN ELEPHANT

The greatest land animal is the African bush elephant. This giant holds other records too, including biggest ears, largest teeth and longest 'nose'.

Elephants are also among the most 'social' animals. They live together in very close-knit groups with a chief female, known as the matriarch, several adult females and their young. Adult males mostly live alone.

LONGEST NOSE

The elephant's trunk has many uses:
★ Breathing
★ Sniffing and smelling
★ Gathering food
★ Stroking babies and other herd members
★ Making trumpet sounds
★ Blowing a 'dust bath'
★ Sucking up water to squirt into the mouth for a drink, or over the body for a cooling shower
★ As a 'snorkel' when swimming

The trunk is the elongated nose and upper lip which have fused, or joined together. It has hundreds of muscles and can bend in any direction.

Tusks are greatly enlarged upper incisor teeth. They grow through life, being larger in males. In an old male, or bull, they can be three metres long. (The narwhal's tusk may be longer but are lighter, see page 56.)

The foot has a springy pad inside, that spreads out to cushion the elephant's weight. This massive creature can walk more silently than most people.

An elephant's skin is almost three centimetres thick and very, very tough.

African elephant
Loxodonta africana

LENGTH	Male up to 7 m
HEIGHT	Male up to 4 m
WEIGHT	Male up to 10 tonnes
RANGE	Africa (south of the Sahara)
DIET	Plants, from roots and bark to buds, leaves and fruits
HABITAT	Grassland, scrub, woods
CONSERVATION STATUS	Vulnerable

A hungry elephant eats more than 250 kilograms of food daily. That's as heavy as four adult humans!

BIG EARS

An elephant's huge ears pick up very faint sounds, such as lions moving nearby. The ears also have many blood vessels and, as they wave, they give off body heat to the air. This prevents the elephant overheating.

FIERCEST FISH

Shark eyes see well only a short distance away. As the shark bites, they roll up into sockets in the head, for protection.

Some teeth are like triangular blades with tiny saw edges for cutting, while others are more pointed for stabbing.

GREAT WHITE SHARK

The great white is armed with razor-sharp teeth and a lethal bite. It has great speed and power, and amazing senses. This super-hunter is the world's largest predatory fish.

Great whites are probably responsible for more attacks on humans than any other sharks. Even so, if you follow a few simple rules, your chances of being bitten are thousands of times less than being hurt in a road accident.

SHARKS' TEETH

Great whites have about 24 teeth in each jaw, upper and lower. Behind each one is a 'queue' of several more teeth. If a front tooth breaks or falls out, the one behind moves into its place. So at any one time, there are 250–300 teeth in total. The replacement happens continually, meaning a great white can have 50,000 teeth through its life.

The nostrils are not passageways, like our own, but bowl-like pits in the nose. They can detect blood in the water several kilometres away.

The snout is covered by hundreds of tiny pits called ampullae. These detect electrical pulses given off naturally by the active muscles of other creatures, even when buried in sand or mud.

Great white shark
Carcharodon carcharias

LENGTH	6-plus m
WEIGHT	Up to 2 tonnes
RANGE	All oceans
DIET	Animals, from whales and seals to seabirds, fish, squid
HABITAT	Coasts, open water
CONSERVATION STATUS	Vulnerable

MAN-EATERS

Apart from great whites, these sharks are known to attack humans:

☆ Bull shark. At 3.5 metres long, it is especially dangerous since it sometimes swims up rivers and into lakes.

☆ Tiger shark. It seems lazy and not bothered, but this 5-metre predator attacks like lightning.

☆ Oceanic white-tip. This 4-metre hunter gathers in a 'feeding frenzy' and bites almost anything that moves.

☆ Great hammerhead. It's a big shark, 6 metres, but its mouth is relatively small.

Sharks have separate gill slits, one for each gill, where the water comes out after passing in through the mouth. The gills take in oxygen from the water.

The great 'white' is only pale or white beneath. Its upper surface is grey, perhaps with a tint of brown, blue or yellow.

STRONGEST BITE

AMERICAN ALLIGATOR

The American alligator may not be quite as big as its cousin, the saltwater crocodile (see page 26). But it is just as fierce, and it has an immense bite that quickly crushes life out of any prey.

Alligators have such mighty mouth-closing muscles, powerful jaws and strong teeth, that they can easily crush the shell of a freshwater turtle or terrapin. But the jaw-opening muscles are so weak, a person could hold the mouth shut. (However, do NOT try this at home!)

CAREFUL MOTHERS

Mother alligators build a mound of rotting plants over their eggs, to keep them warm. As the babies hatch, the mother digs them out and even carries them to water gently in her huge mouth.

'Gators and crocs swallow stones into the stomach, to help them float low in the water and be less noticed from the bank.

The jaws have a total of up to 80 teeth at any one time.

SUPERSIZED SKULL

In prehistoric times, alligators and crocodiles grew even bigger and their bites were even harder!

☆ Purussaurus – 10 metres long, lived 8 million years ago in South America.

☆ Deinosuchus – 11 metres long, lived 75 million years ago in North America (right, attacking an Albertosaurus).

☆ Sarcosuchus – 12 metres long, lived 110 million years ago in Africa.

The alligator has the most powerful bite of any animal tested so far. It's twice as strong as a hyaena's, almost four times a great white's, and nearly ten times our own.

The tail makes up about half of the alligator's total length. It lashes from side to side, to provide the main forward thrust when swimming.

DEATH ROLL

Alligators and crocs use a 'death roll' to tackle big prey. They grab a big chunk of flesh and then twist or spin around along their length, like a twirling ballet dancer, to tear off a swallow-sized piece.

American alligator
Alligator mississippiensis

LENGTH	Up to 5 m, usually 3.5 m
WEIGHT	Up to 1 tonne, usually 300–400 kg
RANGE	South-east North America
DIET	Animals, from fish and turtles to birds, deer, even bears
HABITAT	Rivers, lakes, swamps, other wetlands
CONSERVATION STATUS	No special status

LONGEST SNAKE

RETICULATED PYTHON

Pythons are large and feared 'constrictor' snakes, who constrict or squeeze the life out of their prey. The Asian reticulated python holds the title of longest snake, and also longest reptile.

Measuring the length of a snake may seem easy. But if it's alive, it doesn't stop squirming - and a large live python is very powerful and dangerous! If the snake has died, its muscles and joints relax and give a false measurement that is too big.

'Reticulated' refers to the skin's net-like lines, patches, spots, squares and diamonds, which give incredible camouflage in a shady forest.

Snakes slide along by curling their bodies from side to side as some belly scales tilt to grip the ground, while others go flat and slide forwards.

LONG AND SHORT

The reticulated python is more than 70 times longer than the world's shortest snake. This is the Barbados thread snake, which is just 10 centimetres in length and as thin as a piece of spaghetti.

TIGHT SQUEEZE

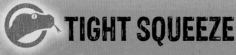

Pythons and boas do not actually crush their prey. Usually they wrap around the victim tightly, and as it breathes out, they tighten their coils slightly. The victim cannot breathe in fully, and this happens several times. Finally the victim cannot breathe at all and dies from suffocation.

The tongue flicks out to catch tiny floating smell particles that are detected in the roof of the mouth.

CLOSE SECOND

The 'biggest' snake, by bulk or weight, is the green anaconda of South American forests, rivers and swamps. It is thicker and more muscular than the reticulated python, around six metres long and weighing up to 100 kilograms.

The mouth can open wide enough to swallow prey the size of wild pigs and goats, small deer, and in one case, a sloth bear!

LONGEST SNAKE

The reticulated python is the length of two Transit vans!

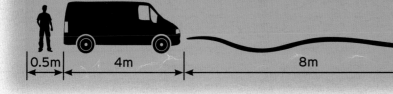

0.5m   4m   8m

BIGGEST BABY

BLUE WHALE CALF

The blue whale is famous as the biggest animal in the whole world (see page 10). Naturally it has the largest baby too – the blue whale calf. This mini-monster is the size of a large family car!

At seven metres, the newborn calf is longer than the smallest type of great whale, the pygmy right whale. This rarely grows longer than six metres.

The mother supports her youngster near the surface with her flippers, as it learns to breathe properly. The calf's blowhole or breathing opening is on top of its head.

HAPPY BIRTHDAY

A baby whale is born tail-first. This means the head comes out last and the baby can then get to the surface quick, to breathe. If the head came out first, the baby might drown while the rest of it waits to emerge.

GROWING BY NUMBERS

30 MINUTES
after birth
FIRST PROPER SWIM

10-12 MONTHS
LEAVES MOTHER

7M
BIRTH LENGTH

2.5 TONNES
BIRTH WEIGHT

40KG
each day
GROWTH (WEIGHT)

3CM
each day
GROWTH (LENGTH)

10 SECONDS
after birth
FIRST BREATH

11-12 MONTHS
PREGNANCY TIME

300 LITRES
per day
MILK INTAKE

The flippers are relatively short in the young whale, compared to the adult.

The calf starts growing fast almost from day one. Every month for the first half-year it becomes one metre longer.

After a few months, the calf begins to filter-feed on plankton from the ocean. By about six months of age it no longer needs its mother's milk.

MOTHER'S MILK

The calf drinks an incredible 300 litres of mother's milk each day – enough to fill four bathtubs! The milk is extremely rich in fats (about half) and nutrients for energy and growth.

COUGH, SPLUTTER!

The calf must learn to swim to the surface to take breaths of air. This means opening its blowhole at just the right time. Sometimes the baby breathes in water, coughs and splutters!

LONGEST TOOTH

THE NARWHAL

Elephants may have the biggest teeth - their tusks. But the narwhal is a rival for the longest tooth.

It grows forward from its mouth as a long, straight, slim, pointed tusk, giving this whale the nickname 'unicorn of the sea'.

The tusk is twisted or helical along its length, almost like a corkscrew.

Narwhals are expert deep divers, sometimes going down more than 1,000 metres to search for prey.

Unlike many whales and dolphins, the narwhal has a smooth back, without a dorsal fin or ridge.

TUSK TALK

A narwhal's tusk is one left upper tooth, a canine, which keeps growing and growing. It is longer in the male than the female. Rarely a narwhal has both a left and a right tusk.

The skin colour gradually becomes paler with age.

GIANT GNASHERS

Several kinds of animals have overgrown teeth that we call tusks.

☆ The heaviest tusks belong to the elephant (see page 47). They weigh up to 100 kilograms each.

☆ The narwhal's tusk is as long but much narrower, weighing 20-25 kilograms.

☆ A walrus has two long tusks which are its upper canine teeth. In big old males they may reach one metre long and weigh five kilograms.

☆ The hippo (right) has lower canine teeth that grow as tusks up to 50 centimetres long.

☆ Male pigs, such as wild boar and warthogs, also have canine tusks.

☆ So do the male small deer called musk deer and water deer.

Narwhal
Monodon monoceros

LENGTH	5 m
WEIGHT	1.5 tonnes
RANGE	Arctic
DIET	Fish, squid, shrimps
TUSK LENGTH	3-plus m
HABITAT	Cold oceans, along coasts, among icebergs
CONSERVATION STATUS	Near threatened

JUST JOUSTING

The narwhal's tusk does not seem to be a proper weapon, or used for feeding. Probably is a sign of the maturity, size and strength of its owner. Male narwhals 'fence' or 'joust' with their tusks, clicking them together to see whose is biggest, and so who's boss.

Small groups of 10-15 narwhals, called pods, swim in formation as they travel.

DEADLIEST SNAKE

ASIAN COBRA

Every year there are more than 50,000 snakebite deaths around the world. The main culprit is probably the Asian cobra.

Many snakes are deadly, but how do you measure the deadliest? That depends on many questions. Is the snake aggressive and likely to bite? There is also the length of its fangs, how hard it bites, the strength of its venom, and how much venom it delivers in the bite. Killing can be so complicated!

Asian cobras live among farms, villages and towns, where they are likely to be disturbed by people, and bite in self defence. This is why they cause so many deaths.

SNAKEBITE ACTION

- Get expert help as fast as possible.
- Use an anti-venom if you have one.
- Keep the victim quiet and still, with the bitten part raised.
- Try to remember a description of the snake, so medical helpers know which venom they are battling.

FANGS AND VENOM

Snakes jab their venom into victims with long, sharp teeth called fangs. In cobras the fangs have a groove along one side or a hole along the middle. This allows the venom to go deep into the victim's flesh, where it causes more damage, faster.

The Asian cobra has two curved marks on its hood, giving it the alternative name of spectacled cobra.

Cobras have two long fangs at the front of the mouth. These normally lie flat along the upper jaw, and swing down to jab in as the snake strikes.

The cobra's hood is spread by tilting its neck ribs under the skin. When the cobra rears up and does this, it means the snake is worried and ready to bite in self defence.

SNAKE STRIKES

☆ One of the most powerful venoms belongs to the Australian inland taipan. It is usually shy and slides away, but it may bite without warning at lightning speed, which makes it double-dangerous.

☆ Sea snakes (below) also have extremely strong venom. But their bites are weak and do not inject much of it, so they rarely cause harm to humans.

☆ The fastest deadly snake is the black mamba. In fact it's the quickest of all snakes, slithering along at five metres per second!

☆ The boomslang, also from Africa, has fangs at the back of its mouth rather than the front. But it still manages to kill people.

Asian cobra
Naja naja

LENGTH	2.2 m
WEIGHT	5-7 kg
RANGE	South Asia
DIET	Small animals such as rats, birds, frogs
HABITAT	Most habitats, from forests to towns
CONSERVATION STATUS	Protected in many countries across its range

The cobra sheds its whole skin with the scales every year or two, even the transparent scale covering each eye.

BIGGEST BEETLE

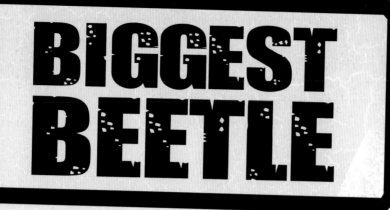

GOLIATH BEETLE

The goliath beetle is a truly heavyweight champion. It weighs as much as 100,000 of its tiniest insect cousins, such as midges or gall-wasps.

Beetles in general hold an amazing record too. They make up the world's largest animal group, with more than 400,000 different kinds - more than one-quarter of all known species.

Male goliaths have a Y-shaped upper snout for pushing each other as they fight at breeding time. Females have a spade-like snout to dig into soil, to lay their eggs.

Each long, strong leg ends in two sharp, pincer-like claws for gripping bark, twigs and even slippery leaves.

LONGEST BODY

★ The beetle with the longest main body is the Hercules beetle of the Americas.

★ It's up to 18 centimetres, including the rhinoceros-like horn, which is much lengthier in males.

★ But this is not the longest of all insects. The giant stick insect from South East Asia called Chan's megastick, including its antennae (feelers), is more than 55 centimetres!

Goliaths are brightly marked with almost-white stripes and patches on a dark brown or black background. Each beetle has its own pattern, like a fingerprint.

TINY COUSINS

Some featherwing beetles are only 1/3rd of one millimetre long – 1/300th the length of their giant goliath cousins, and as small as this full stop. Each of the beetle's flying wings is a stalk with lots of hairs on either side, similar to a bird's feather. Neat!

A beetle's tough, shield-like back is actually its thick, hard front wings, called elytra. These tilt up and sideways to reveal the flight wings, which unfold from beneath.

Goliath beetle
Goliathus (several kinds)

LENGTH	Up to 10 cm
WEIGHT	More than 100 g
RANGE	Africa
DIET	Plant juices, buds, fruits
HABITAT	Mostly forests, woods
CONSERVATION STATUS	No special status

DEADLIEST DEFENCE

The bombardier beetle looks small and peaceful. But when in danger, it bends its body around to spray horrible burning gases from its rear end. The gases come from two substances made separately inside the body, which mix as they emerge with a tiny explosion.

BIGGEST BUTTERFLY

QA BIRDWING

Is it a bird, or even a small plane? No, it's the beautiful Queen Alexandra's birdwing, the world's largest butterfly. This delicate giant is found only on the island of New Guinea, South East Asia.

Like many butterflies, male and female birdwings look different. Females are larger, with more rounded wings coloured in shades of dark and light brown.

Females look for male QA birdwings, whose territories consist of patches of rainforest trees. Males flap at and chase off other males who come near.

WONDERFUL WINGS

Butterflies and moths have thousands of tiny leaf-like scales on their wings. These microscales are different colours, and they angle and overlap in various ways. This gives the wings a beautiful glowing sheen that is iridescent, changing hue with the angle of view.

Unlike this female, the male has shiny blue green wings with dark brown streaks, and his body is bright yellow.

QA birdwing
Ornithoptera alexandrae

LENGTH	Up to 10 cm
WINGSPAN	More than 30 cm
WEIGHT	12 g
RANGE	Papua New Guinea
DIET	Caterpillars eat vine sap, buds, flowers and bark; adults sip flower nectar
HABITAT	Tropical forest, scrub
CONSERVATION STATUS	Endangered

SPOT-THE-DIFFERENCE

No single feature is the difference between moths and butterflies. But in general:

★ Most moths fly at night, and most butterflies by day.

★ Many moths have hairy bodies, most butterflies have smooth ones.

★ Moths usually rest with wings to the side, butterflies hold their wings together over the back.

★ Moths have feathery antennae (feelers), butterflies have thin antennae with clubbed tips.

Butterflies have a long feeding tube called a proboscis. This usually coils under the head, then extends like a drinking straw to sip nectar.

GIANT AND PYGMY

Some moths rival Queen Alexandra's birdwing. The Atlas moth of South East Asia and the Hercules moth from Australia both have wings almost 30 centimetres across. At the other end of the size scale, the western pygmy blue butterfly in North America is as small as a fingernail.

The wingspan of the male is 16–20 cm, compared to this female's 30-plus cm.

BIGGEST SQUID

COLOSSAL SQUID

Is it giant or colossal? That's very important when dealing with deep-sea monsters. The giant squid was long believed to be the biggest invertebrate (animal without a backbone). But then ...

... Experts checked some old "giant" squid and new catches, and found they were a different kind, or species – the colossal squid. This is truly giant...er...colossal... hmm...mammoth?

There are eight medium-sized tentacles and two very long ones, all for catching prey.

MONSTERS FROM THE DEEP

Old-time sailors feared a great beast that came from the ocean depths, pulled their ship apart, and ate them one by one. In the far North, this vast monster was called the kraken. The legends are probably based on sightings of giant and colossal squid. Kraken often star in adventure films such as *Pirates of the Caribbean*.

A squid's mouth is in the centre at the base of the tentacles. It is hard, hooked and horny, like a parrot's bill.

MASSIVE CATCHES

Colossal and giant squid are among the top predators in their deep-sea world, and so rare. But with modern fishing methods, more are being found. In 2007 the biggest colossal squid studied so far, weighing half a tonne, was caught alive in the Ross Sea, Antarctica.

The squid's main body is covered by a cloak-like mantle with wide fins at the end for swimming.

Colossal squid
Mesonychoteuthis hamiltoni

LENGTH	Up to 14 m including tentacles
WEIGHT	500 kg, probably more
RANGE	Cool southern oceans
DIET	Other squid, fish, similar creatures
HABITAT	Deep sea
CONSERVATION STATUS	No special status

EYE-EYE!

Seeing in the dark depths means colossal and giant squid have the world's largest eyes. These are more than 25 cm across – bigger than a soccer ball.

The tentacles have strong suckers and fierce, sharp hooks that grab and pull victims to the mouth.

SMALLEST CRAB

Pea crab

Pinnotheres pisum

WIDTH	5-7 mm
RANGE	Europe
DIET	Steals food from host
HABITAT	Coasts and shallow seas
CONSERVATION STATUS	No special status

PEA CRAB

All crabs start off tiny, as eggs, and grow up by shedding their shells every few weeks or months. But the pea crab soon stops growing. Even when adult, it is only the size of a green pea. Cute!

Pea crabs are so small, they can easily get inside the shells or bodies of other creatures, such as mussels and clams. This is where they live as unwanted guests called parasites.

BIGGEST CRAB

The Japanese spider crab is a true monster. It has a body the size of a dinner plate, four pairs of long spindly legs, and - in the male - enormously long pincers. These stretch out to measure more than three metres across.

Pea crabs have a rounded body, mini-pincers and tiny short legs. Once safe inside their host, they do not have to travel far or defend themselves.

The crab's main shell is called its carapace. In a young crab it is almost see-through, showing the heart, guts, gills and other parts inside.

BEST BOXER

Boxer or pom-pom crabs hold a sea anemone in each pincer, like flowery boxing gloves. The anemones have venom stings and so other creatures keep away from the crab, while the crab helps the anemone to catch prey.

The crab steals food and nutrients from its host. At the same time the host gets very irritated but usually cannot get rid of its parasite.

This pea crab's host is a heart urchin. Other hosts include sea-squirts, sponges, sea cucumbers and even bigger crabs!

ROBBER! THIEF!

Along Asian and Pacific coasts, the robber crab or coconut crab is a real tough landlubber. It is at home out of water, walks along paths, and even climbs up trees and onto house roofs. This fruit-eater has legs almost one metre across. Never mess with it or you'll get a truly fierce pinch!

GREATEST GROWTH SPURT

OCEAN SUNFISH

Nearly all fish start off as tiny eggs. The ocean sunfish does too, but its rate of growth is amazing. In its first year it grows 1,000 times in size, and then several hundred times as big for a few more years.

This ocean giant is the world's largest bony fish. (Some sharks are bigger but they have cartilage skeletons.) It's also one of the few fish that's taller than it is long.

Instead of the usual fishy tail (caudal fin), the sunfish has a wrap-around fleshy ''frill' called the clavus.

PRICKLY BABIES

The fry, or newly-hatched young, of sunfish have spines like their close relations, the pufferfish and porcupinefish.

The tall fins on the top and bottom of the body are the dorsal and anal fins. The fish swims along by waving them slowly.

ALL-DAY BREAKFASTS

Most sunfish food is not very nourishing –
jellyfish, seaweed, and perhaps a few hard
shellfish and crabs. So this huge fish eats for
many hours every day, tearing up meals with its
hard, beak-like mouth.

Ocean sunfish
Mola mola

LENGTH	May be over 3 m
HEIGHT	Can be more than 4 m
WEIGHT	Up to 2 tonnes
RANGE	Tropical and warm waters worldwide
DIET	Jellyfish, other sea creatures
HABITAT	Open ocean
CONSERVATION STATUS	No special status

Sunfish sometimes rest on
their sides, lying at or near
the surface. Whether they
are tired, feeling ill, or
enjoying a sunbathe,
nobody knows.

SCALE-LESS SUPER-SKIN

A sunfish has tough, leathery skin up to eight centimetres
thick. This is covered, not in big scales like other fish, but
by an extra-thick layer of gooey slime.

The body is like a circle or
oval, but very thin from side
to side. Head-on, the sunfish
looks super-slim!

SUPERSIZED SHELL

GIANT CLAM

Bulkier than a suitcase, and as heavy as three people, the giant clam is the largest shellfish with the world's biggest shell.

Some people like to eat shellfish such as mussels, oysters and clams. The giant clam would provide a huge meal – but it is rare due to problems like collecting for food and trophies, pollution and global warming. So it's now protected by law in many places.

The shell has wavy ridges or corrugations. These make it much stronger, for the same amount of shell material, than a smooth shell.

LUSCIOUS LIPS

Clams don't kiss! The bright "lips" are the body part called the mantle. They contain thousands of speck-sized plants, algae, that use sunlight to make their own food. They share some of this with the clam, and in return, they receive a safe home. This two-way benefit is known as mutualism.

SPEEDIEST SHELLFISH

Most shellfish lie still on rocks or the sea bed. But the scallop can flap its two valves fast to squirt water from between them. This sends it jerkily speeding along at up to one metre per second.

LENGTH	120 cm
WIDTH	50 cm when almost closed
WEIGHT	More than 200 kg
RANGE	Indian and West Pacific Oceans
DIET	Tiny floating animals, plants and nutrient particles
HABITAT	Shallow, clear, clean water
LIFESPAN	Over 120 years
CONSERVATION STATUS	Vulnerable

The clam feeds by passing sea water over its slime-covered fringed gills, inside the shell. Tiny floating bits of food stick to the slime and go into the stomach.

The frilly, colourful mantle produces new hard material to make the shell larger each year. Big giant clams are very old!

Shellfish shells are made mainly from the mineral calcium carbonate (also in limestone and chalk), plus substances like chitin, which also forms the hard outer casings of insects.

PERFECT PEARL

The record-breaking pearl known as the Pearl of Lao Tze came from a giant clam. It's 24 centimetres long and weighs 6.4 kilograms. But it's not round and "pearly" like a proper oyster pearl, it is lumpy and shiny white. Shellfish make a pearl when a bit of grit gets inside their shell, and they produce a milky mineral as protection to "wall it off."

PRETTIEST DISGUISE

ORCHID MANTIS

Keen to drink nectar, the butterfly buzzes down to a beautifully coloured flower with delicate petals. SNAP! On the flower is an orchid mantis, which grabs the victim with its spiky jacknife front legs.

There are many kinds of flower mantises in tropical Africa and Asia. Each one seeks out flowers with shapes and colours to match itself, so it can wait unnoticed.

Mantises have wings, and males can usually fly well.

As the mantis grows, it takes on the main colour of flowers in its area – white, pink, purple, yellow or green.

The two rear pairs of legs have wide flaps, exactly like flower petals.

MATES FOR DINNER

The female mantis is much larger than the male. At mating time he must be very careful and get away quickly. Otherwise, if she is hungry, she may eat him!

Mantises have huge eyes and fabulous eyesight. They can spot even tiny meals such as midges and gnats.

MASTERS OF DISGUISES

Looking like your surroundings is known as camouflage. Insects like the Luna moth (below) have many astonishing examples of this disguise. You can probably guess what each of these creatures looks like!

☆ The dead-leaf katydid
☆ Stick- and twig-insects
☆ The bird-dropping caterpillar

The mantis is one of very few insects with a moveable neck, allowing it to look around for food and danger.

The two front legs fold back on themselves, with fierce spikes that stab into the prey.

Orchid mantis
Hymenopus coronatus

LENGTH	Female 5-6 cm; male 2-3 cm
WEIGHT	5-7 g
RANGE	South East Asia
DIET	Small creatures, occasionally fruits
HABITAT	Forests, shrubs
CONSERVATION STATUS	No special status

PREYING, NOT PRAYING

These insects are sometimes called "praying mantises" because they hold their front legs up and together, as people hold their hands in prayer. Maybe the mantis prays for prey?

BOGGLIEST EYES

LENGTH	40 cm
WEIGHT	200-plus g
RANGE	East Africa
DIET	Small creatures like insects, spiders, worms, also fruits, plant food
HABITAT	Woods, shrubs
HORNS	Present only in males
CONSERVATION STATUS	No special status

THREE HORNED CHAMELEON

Look over here, to the front left – and there, to the rear right! Impossible for us to do at the same time. But for a chameleon, no problem!

Chameleons are tree-dwelling lizards. More than 160 kinds live in the warmer parts of Europe, Africa and Asia.

LONG TONGUE, STICKY TIP

The chameleon holds the record for tongue length compared to body length. It's usually squashed inside the mouth. To catch a meal the tongue flicks out, its gummy tip sticks to the victim, and the tongue shoots back into the mouth – all faster than you can see.

"I'M IN A MOOD!"

Chameleons famously change skin colour to tell other chameleons about their moods and intentions. Very dark means: "Watch out, I'm angry!" Light and patchy says: "Be my mate!" At other times the colours are for camouflage or body temperature control.

To help climbing, the chameleon's tail curls around and grasps twigs and branches. This type of gripping tail is known as prehensile.

Some chameleons, like the usambara, have three long horns, one on the nose-tip and one above each eye.

Each eye moves on its own, so the chameleon can look in two directions at once and go cross-eyed on purpose. This helps to detect prey and enemies anywhere around.

The pincer-like feet grip even tiny twigs tightly for hours without getting tired. On each foot, each side of the "pincer" is made of two or three toes joined together.

RECORD COLOUR-CHANGER

Chameleon colour changes take minutes, even hours. They cannot match cuttlefish and squid. These sea creatures flash amazing patterns along their bodies, including black-and-white zebra-stripes, red blotches, green spots and brown patches – many times each second!

PRICKLIEST CHARACTER

COMMON PORCUPINE

Shuffle, snort, shake, rattle, stroll – the porcupine rarely hurries. It knows that very few animals try to attack because its long spines, called quills, are superb defence.

More than 30 kinds of porcupines live across the Americas, Africa and Asia. They are rodents with long gnawing front teeth, related to beavers, rats and squirrels.

MORE SPIKY CREATURES

Various animals have quills, spikes and spines for protection. They include hedgehogs (below), sea-urchins, crown-of-thorns starfish and lionfish. The porcupinefish (right) swallows water to make its body bigger so its spikes stand out.

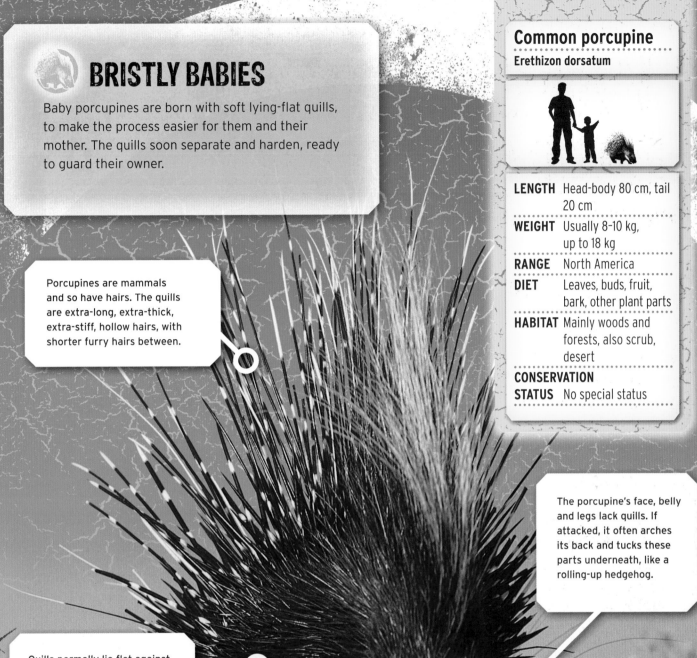

BRISTLY BABIES

Baby porcupines are born with soft lying-flat quills, to make the process easier for them and their mother. The quills soon separate and harden, ready to guard their owner.

Porcupines are mammals and so have hairs. The quills are extra-long, extra-thick, extra-stiff, hollow hairs, with shorter furry hairs between.

The porcupine's face, belly and legs lack quills. If attacked, it often arches its back and tucks these parts underneath, like a rolling-up hedgehog.

Quills normally lie flat against the body. When in danger, they stick out and rattle in a display of defence, making the porcupine look big and fierce.

QUESTION OF QUILLS

The common porcupine has more than 25,000 quills up to 15 cm long. It cannot shoot them like arrows from a bow. But it can swing around and jab them into the enemy. The barbed tips stick into the flesh, and the quills come away as the porcupine moves off. Getting them out hurts!

Porcupines have strong feet and climb well. On the ground, if their defence display does not work against a predator, they gallop to the nearest tree and clamber into the branches.

HIGHEST JUMPER

MEADOW FROGHOPPER

The meadow froghopper is a small bug that hangs around on plant stems and buds, sucking juicy sap. Yet for its size, this dull-looking creature is the world's greatest animal leaper!

Adult froghoppers can spring straight up more than 70 centimetres, which outleaps the best fleas at 30-40 centimetres. Also the froghopper is heavier than the flea, making its feat even more amazing!

Like most insects, froghoppers have wings and they can fly, as well as glide down from their tremendous leaps.

COVERED IN SPIT!

Froghoppers are also called spitbugs or spittlebugs. During the early stage in their life, called the nymph or larva, they cover themselves with a bubbly foam, to protect them from cold and heat, and to hide from predators. Country folk call the froth cuckoo spit or frog spit.

FORMER RECORD-HOLDER

Pity the poor flea! This pesky blood-sucking insect held the highest jumper record for many years, until scientific tests in 2009 showed the froghopper is the real champion.

Bugs like the froghopper have sharp, drawn-out, beak-like mouthparts. These pierce plants and suck up sweet juices containing high-energy sugars.

Big boggly eyes on the side of the head give the insect the 'frog' part of its name.

The froghopper's two rear legs are so long and specialized that they drag behind during normal walking, which the bug does using its front and middle pairs.

WHAT A BOUND!

★ The froghopper can jump 70 cm straight up, which is 100 times its body length.

★ That's like an adult human leaping over a 50-floor skyscraper - half the height of New York's Empire State Building!

★ As it takes off, the froghopper experiences 400g (400 times the force of gravity). That's 100 times the g-force suffered by human astronauts at blast-off, and 200 times what you might feel for a second or two on a fast rollercoaster.

Meadow froghopper
Philaenus spumarius

LENGTH	5-7 mm
WEIGHT	12 mg (0.012 g)
RANGE	Most of Northern Hemisphere
DIET	Sap and other plant juices
JUMP	Height 70 cm
CONSERVATION STATUS	No special status

BEST BUILDER

AMERICAN BEAVER

Beavers are nature's master builders. They construct huge dams to hold back stream water and make a pool, and make domed lodges in the pool as home for their family. Their materials are totally natural – wood, mud and stone.

These toothy, furry creatures are rodents, in the same mammal group as rats, mice and squirrels. Their main construction tools are the long gnawing front teeth that all rodents have, and their hand-like front paws.

ALL DAMMED UP

The beavers pile up and interlock twigs and branches, weigh them down with pebbles and stones, and plug the gaps with earth and mud. This makes a waterproof wall, and dammed water forms a pool or lake for their lodge. The longest known beaver dam measured over 800 metres!

The beaver's thick furry coat keeps it warm even when swimming in icy water during midwinter.

TOOTHY TOOLS

Beavers gnash and gnaw trees for food and also for building materials. They chew around the trunk low down so the tree topples. Then they can eat the soft leaves and bark that were out of reach, and cut off branches for their dam and lodge.

Very long whiskers on the face help the beaver to feel its way at night, when it's most active on land and in water.

The nostrils, eyes and ears are on top of the head, so a beaver can swim almost submerged but still breathe, see and hear.

The front paws are like hands to handle building materials, while the rear ones are webbed for swimming.

American beaver
Castor canadensis

SIZE	Head-body 70-90 cm
TAIL	Length 35-45 cm, width 15 cm
WEIGHT	Up to 40 kg
RANGE	North and South America
DIET	Plants, especially soft bark and juicy wood
HABITAT	Woods and forests with waterways, pools, streams
CONSERVATION STATUS	No special status

LODGE LIVING

The beaver family home is made in a similar way to the dam, with a thick wolf-proof roof and lynx-proof underwater entrance. Inside are platforms above the water surface where the beavers store food, groom their all-important thick fur, relax and sleep in safety.

OLDEST LANDLUBBER

GIANT TORTOISE

Tortoises are exceedingly well-shelled, extremely slow – and exceptionally long-lived. They are the main contenders for the oldest land creature on Earth.

But it's tricky to keep track of one tortoise for hundreds of years. Who knows whether, if one dies, another similar tortoise might not sneakily be put in its place, to keep the record going? The same might happen with parrots, fish and other oldest-ever contestants.

Giant tortoises feed on many different plant foods, including leaves, grass, flowers, fruits, seeds, vegetables, berries and even prickly cactus.

Giant tortoise

Dipsochelys, Aldabrachelys (Aldabra), Chelonoidis (Galapagos)

LENGTH	Shell 120 cm, overall 180 cm
WEIGHT	Up to 400 kg
RANGE	Islands of Indian and Pacific Oceans
DIET	Varied plants, from soft fruits to thorny cactus
HABITAT	Varied, from cool grasslands to cactus scrub, woods, parks
CONSERVATION STATUS	Vulnerable;

MEGA-SHELLS

The upper domed part of the shell is the carapace. It has an outer layer of horn-like plates made of keratin (like our fingernails), called scutes, with a layer of bony plates beneath. The flat shell base is known as the plastron. Like the carapace it has horny scutes that grow in the skin, covering bony plates.

LONG-LIFE LAND RECORDS

How do tortoises measure up to other land animals with extreme lifespans?

☆ Human - 122 years maximum.
☆ Tuatara (lizard-like New Zealand reptile) - 120 years.
☆ Asian elephant - 86 years.
☆ Cockatoo - 78 years.
☆ Albatross - 60-plus years.

Water creatures like the water dragon (left) are even longer-lived than land ones. They include certain whales, koi carp and the current record-holder, the ocean quahog, or hard clam.

The skin on the head, neck and legs grows protective scales, as in other reptiles.

Tortoises have a toothless, sharp-edged, beak-like mouth to chop up plant food.

CHAMPION CONTENDER AGES

☆ Adwaita, an Aldabran giant tortoise - at least 150 years, possibly 250. Died in Kolkata, India in 2006.
☆ Tu'i Malila, a radiated tortoise - probably 188 or 189 years old. Died in Tonga in 1965.
☆ Harriet, a Galapagos giant tortoise - estimated 175 years. Died in Australia in 2006.
☆ Jonathan, a Seychelles giant tortoise - hatched from his egg in 1832 and still going! He lives on St Helena island in the Atlantic.

Tortoises are famously slow and usually saunter along at less than 10 metres each minute. In a hurry, they "sprint" at one metre every 5-8 seconds.

MOST SKILLFUL SPINNER

GOLDEN SILK ORB-WEAVER

Orb-weavers are the supreme silk-spinners of the spider world. Their circular webs stretch across paths, clearings, streams, openings and any other gaps where prey might fly by.

It takes a typical orb-weaver one or two hours to construct its web. It climbs to a place just above and upwind of the gap, makes a light silk line, and waits for the breeze to float this across. When the line catches and sticks on the other side, the spider tightrope-walks part-way along, floats more lines across, and so on.

SPIDER SILK

Spider silks are made in several sets of silk glands, in the rear body. The liquid silk squirts out through small holes at the ends of up to eight finger-like parts known as spinnerets. The spider's rear legs twist, squeeze and extend the silk as it dries in air, to form stretchy strands.

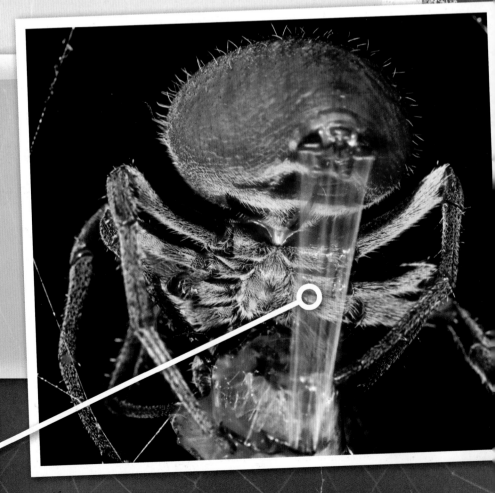

When prey are plentiful, the spider wraps them in silk and stores them near the web, still alive, to eat later.

 NEW WEBS FOR OLD

★ Orb-weavers build a new web almost every day.

★ If a big prey like a bird or bat, or perhaps heavy rain, causes damage, the spider repairs this as soon as possible.

★ The spider nearly always eats the old silk, to use the nutrients again. It's an amazing example of natural recycling!

Golden silk orb-weaver

Nephila (many species)

LENGTH	Head-body up to 6 cm, leg span up to 14 cm
RANGE	Worldwide in warmer regions
DIET	Small animals, from flies to birds and bats
HABITAT	Woods, forests, parks, wetlands
WEB	Total size up to 4 m wide and tall; central orb up to 2 m across
CONSERVATION STATUS	No special status

The spider may wait on its web centre. Or it could be hidden nearby, with a foot on the web strands to feel if a victim arrives.

Golden orb-weavers are named from the yellow or orange-tinged silk in their webs. The spiders themselves are mostly green, yellow or red with a white patch on the back, and striped legs.

The central web is not a series of circles, but one long spiral of sticky silk, going round and getting smaller from edge to centre.

The standard orb web has spokes called radials, spreading out from the centre or hub. Guy lines around the edge keep it pulled taut.

 NEW ORB-WEAVER FINDS

★ Komac's golden orb-weaver was only identified in 2000. It is the largest of the orb-weaver group, lives in Madagascar and South Africa, and makes webs one metre across.

★ Another recent discovery is Darwin's bark spider, also from Madagascar. Its giant webs are almost two metres across, with guy lines stretching 10 metres on either side!

FASTEST VENOM

BOX-JELLYFISH

Measuring the deadliness of venomous animals is difficult. But at or near the top of the list is the box-jellyfish, also called the sea-wasp.

It would certainly win a prize for fastest-acting venom. From being stung to being dead can take as little as as three minutes.

 ## MICRO-STINGERS

The tiny stingers on jellyfish tentacles are known as cnidocytes. Each has a microscopic dagger-like barb that shoots out from a cup-shaped container as if on a coiled spring. This stabs into the victim, then venom pumps into the wound.

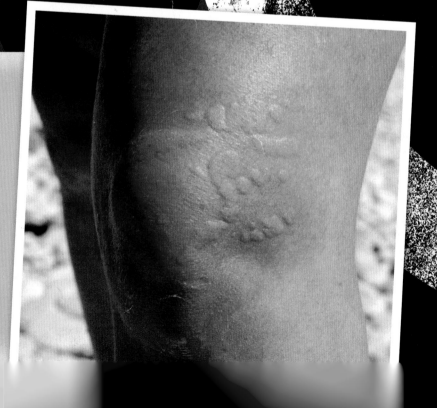

The box-jellyfish's main body, or bell, is shaped like a narrow umbrella. It can expand and contract, called "pulsing", to draw in and then squirt out water, and so push itself along.

The four sets of tentacles, 15 in each set, are more than 3 metres long when they extend and trail behind the body.

In bunches around the edge of the body are a total of 24 simple eyes. They detect patches of light and dark. So the jellyfish can swim, for example, away from dark rocks and towards the lighter open sea.

The tentacles catch creatures such as fish, then contract to move the prey to the mouth in the main body.

Each tentacle has more than half a million micro-stingers called cnidocytes to jab in killer venom.

Box-jellyfish
Chironex fleckeri and others

LENGTH	3-plus m with tentacles extended
BODY SIZE	Main body or bell 30 cm across
WEIGHT	Up to 5 kg
RANGE	South East Asia, Australia
DIET	Small fish, shrimps, prawns
HABITAT	Coastal water and open ocean
CONSERVATION STATUS	No special status

MASS KILLER

☆ Box-jellyfish venom causes terrible stinging pain and burning feelings within seconds.

☆ It then affects the heart and nerves, with yet more agonizing pain and muscle spasms.

☆ If a person touches more than about 3 metres in combined length of tentacles, death is more likely.

☆ The heartbeat becomes unsteady and the heart may stop altogether, called cardiac arrest.

☆ One jellyfish has enough venom in all its tentacles to kill more than 50 humans.

BIGGEST HOME

GREAT BARRIER REEF

A single coral creature, a polyp, is about the size of this "o". But millions of them, working for thousands of years, have created the biggest animal-made structure on Earth – Australia's Great Barrier Reef. This reef is about 20,000 years old, but it grew on an older one that started half a million years ago, then died due to natural climate change.

The stone skeletons of corals build up over many years in various shapes and patterns, depending on the type of polyp. Older coral structures crack and fall apart, making yet more hidey-holes.

STONY SKELETONS

Many kinds of polyp take minerals from the water to construct hard containers or outer skeletons. Shaped like bowls or cups, these give strength and protection to their soft bodies. When each polyp dies, another builds its skeleton on top, and so the structure grows.

Colourful fish, like these coral rabbitfish, love the rocky reef's caves, ledges, nooks and crannies. They can lurk and wait for small prey, or dash in to hide from enemies.

RECORD-BREAKER REEF

☆ The Great Barrier Reef stretches for 2,500 kilometres along Australia's north-east coast.

☆ It consists of a long chain of almost 1,000 islands and 3,000 individual reefs.

☆ The reef is between 15 and 150 km from the shore.

☆ Its width varies from 25 km in the north to over 200 km in the south.

☆ It has more than 400 species of reef-building corals.

☆ Also 1,500 kinds of fish, 200 types of birds, 5,000 species of shellfish and other molluscs, six types of sea turtles...

PRETTY POLYP

What are coral polyps? A polyp is a small sea creature related to jellyfish and anemones. Like an anemone, it has a stalked body and stinging tentacles to catch tiny prey. Most also have plant-like microbes in their bodies, zooxanthellae. These catch sunlight to make their own food, and share it with the polyp.

The dot-dash butterflyfish has a stripe over its eye and an orange tail base, to make predators wonder which end is which – head or tail?

SNEAKIEST FISH

STONEFISH

Is the stonefish the world's most poisonous fish? No. But it is the most venomous fish. Every year people die in terrible pain from its powerful venom. The stonefish could also win prizes for best camouflage and ugliest fish!

Venom is a substance jabbed or stabbed into the victim from the outside. The stonefish does this with sharp spines on its back. Poison is a substance in an animal or plant, that another creature eats and which affects it from the inside.

The venom comes from bag-like glands at the base of the fin spines.

PUFFERFISH

The stonefish is not poisonous, but the pufferfish certainly is! Some of its body parts, including the skin and liver, contain the second most powerful poison in the world, after the golden poison frog (page 96). Even so, daring people cut out non-poisonous parts to cook and eat. If they make a mistake, they could die in agonizing pain.

Lying still on the sea bed, the stonefish's lumpy body, wide fins, mottled pattern and dark colours all combine to make it look exactly like seaweedy rocks and pebbles.

STONEFISH SPINES

Usually the stonefish keeps its spines folded down on its back. The 12-14 spines are part of the dorsal fin. If danger comes near, the fish tilts the spines up so they point at the enemy, ready to inject venom.

The bulging eyes on top of the head look upwards from the ocean floor, keeping watch for food and danger.

Stonefish

Synanceia horrida, S. verrucosa, others

LENGTH	Up to 50 cm
WEIGHT	2-2.5 kg
RANGE	Coasts of South and South East Asia, Australia
DIET	Fish, shrimps, other small creatures
HABITAT	Shallow seas, reefs, estuaries
CONSERVATION STATUS	No special status

MORE SPINY VENOMS

Several other fish have venomous spines to protect themselves against predators. The weeverfish has spines on its back and also its gill covers. It lies almost buried in sand, watching for prey, its spines ready just in case.

The fish's big, upturned mouth is ideal to gulp in unsuspecting prey such as small fish that swim just above.

BIGGEST KILLER

Mosquitoes are flies, which means they have only two wings. (Most insects have four wings.)

ANOPHELES MOSQUITO

Which animal is the world's biggest killer of humans? Not the shark, the tiger or the hippo. This awful record goes to a small insect – the mosquito.

The blood-sucking bites of mosquitoes spread diseases that kill millions of people every year.

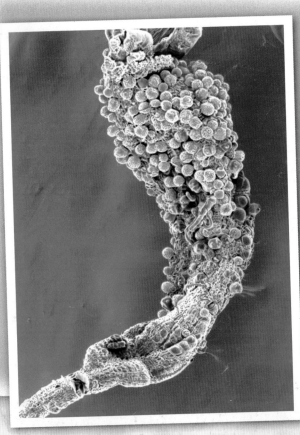

As the mosquito sucks, her rear body or abdomen swells hugely with the red blood inside.

SPIT IT OUT

When a mosquito bites someone with malaria, it takes in blood with the tiny parasites, called Plasmodium. These multiply and form eggs (blue on a mosquito's stomach, left) and young. At the next bite, some parasites in the mosquito's saliva (spit) get into the new victim, passing on the disease.

LIFE CYCLE

Like many insects, a mosquito has four stages in its life.

☆ Eggs are laid by the female on, in or near water.

☆ Eggs hatch into wriggly larvae (grubs) that live in water.

☆ The larva develops a hard outer case and becomes an inactive pupa.

☆ Out of the pupa comes the adult – the buzzy little fly that we swat if it comes near.

The feathery antennae (feelers) have sensors to detect carbon dioxide. This gas is breathed out by animals, including humans, and is how the mozzy finds its victim.

The long, needle-like mouthparts slice easily into a victim's skin, to reach tiny blood vessels beneath. The bite injects saliva which contains substances to prevent blood clotting.

DEADLY DIET

Only female mosquitoes suck blood. They need the blood nutrients for their eggs to develop. Male mozzies feed on nectar and other plant juices.

Anopheles mosquito
Anopheles gambiae, others

LENGTH	6-8 mm
WEIGHT	0.3 mg
RANGE	Mainly tropical areas
DIET	Blood for female
HABITAT	Most habitats, but needs water to breed
CONSERVATION STATUS	No special status

MOST MASSIVE MEAT-EATER

POLAR BEAR

The biggest and most powerful predators on land are not lions, or even tigers – they are bears. Polar bears and brown or grizzly bears share this size record.

However there's a big difference. Brown bears are omnivores – they have a hugely varied diet, including fruits, roots, nuts and honey. Polar bears are much more carnivorous, eating almost nothing but meat.

TINY BABIES

Like other bears, the polar bear mother gives birth to relatively tiny babies. Each new cub is as small as an adult person's clenched fist. It weighs only one kilogram, which is just 0.3% of its mother's weight. In humans this proportion is nearer 5%, and in the shingleback lizard 33%!

The bear's superb sense of smell can detect a seal hiding in the snow more than one kilometre away. If the wind is right, it can sniff out a dead whale at a distance of 10 kilometres!

Vast paws, bigger than dinner plates, help to spread the polar bear's weight on soft snow. And they work as wide paddles when swimming.

Polar bear
Ursus maritimus

LENGTH	3 m
HEIGHT	Stands up to 2.5 m
WEIGHT	Males more than 750 kg
RANGE	Arctic
DIET	Seals, whales, fish
SPEED	Running 30 km/h swimming 10 km/h
CONSERVATION STATUS	Vulnerable

BIGGER AND BIGGER

★ Polar bears on land cannot compare to the sea's fearsome, clever and cunning hunter - the killer whale or orca. Big males are 9 metres long and weigh in at 10 tonnes.

★ Yet the killer whale is dwarfed by the planet's mega-predator - the sperm whale. It grows to a seriously whopping 20 metres and 50 tonnes.

★ The sperm whale hunts the biggest prey too - giant and colossal squid. They weigh half a tonne, with a total length of 12-plus metres.

The polar bear has fur 15 centimetres long, and 10 centimetres of fatty blubber under its skin. If the temperature rises above 10°C, it starts to suffer heatstroke!

BIN-BAG BEARS

As polar bears move along the shore, and across sea ice, they pass coastal towns. Some hungry bears learn to raid rubbish bins and sniff around trash heaps for thrown-away food and leftovers. This can be very dangerous since if the bear is disturbed by people, it may attack.

DEADLIEST FROG

GOLDEN POISON FROG

The golden poison frog doesn't look very harmful. In fact, to many people it appears quite cute. But do not touch! This small, bright amphibian has enough poison to kill up to 20 people!

The frog's bright colour warns other creatures not to eat or even touch it or others of its kind. Even the slightest touch can greatly harm humans and animals.

DARTS AND ARROWS

Several kinds of small poisonous frogs are used by local people in South America to help their hunting. The sharp points of arrows or blowpipe darts are rubbed onto the frog, to coat them with the poison. Then any animal that falls victim to the hunters is likely to die very quickly, rather than be wounded and escape.

The poison is in tiny glands in the frog's skin, especially on its back and neck. It affects nerves and muscles causing muscle spasms, paralysis, breathing problems and heart stoppage.

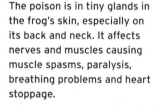

TOO SMALL TO SEE

The frog's poison is so powerful that just a thousandth of one gram can kill a person. That's as much as is contained in a couple of drops the size of salt grains.

Golden poison frog
Phyllobates terribilis

LENGTH	Head-body 5-6 cm
RANGE	North-west South America
DIET	Ants, beetles, worms, other small creatures
HABITAT	Tropical rainforest
POISON	Batrachotoxins
CONSERVATION STATUS	Endangered

Like other frogs, the golden poison frog has huge eyes that are excellent at seeing small, fast-moving objects such as flies and ants.

The skin poison is used as self-defence. Creatures who try to eat these frogs suffer greatly and quickly learn to leave them alone.

KILLER PETS?

It's thought that the golden poison frog does not make the poison itself, in its own body. It probably comes from the frog's food in the wild - especially small flower beetles. Golden poison frogs that are hatched and brought up in captivity, and fed different foods, do not have the deadly skin poison.

Sticky pads on the fingers and toes allow the frog to climb wet, slippery leaves and bark in its rainforest home.

LOUDEST VOICE

HOWLER MONKEY

Did you hear that howler monkey? I said: "DID YOU HEAR THAT HOWLER?" This monkey makes the loudest noise of any land animal, echoing across the forest at dawn and dusk.

Howlers make a variety of noises. Loudest is the howling roar that tells other animals: "This is my patch of forest." Other sounds include screeches warning of danger, clicks, grunts and barks.

NOISY CRITTERS

Sound volume or loudness is measured in decibels, dB. Measuring animals in this way is difficult, but here are some averages for land creatures:

☆ Elephant trumpet - 110 dB
☆ Cicada (a bug, right) - 115 dB
☆ Human shout - 120 dB
☆ Lion roar - 125 dB
☆ Howler howl - 130 dB
☆ Loudest is the blue whale in water (see page 10) - 188 dB.

LOVE SONGS

In South East Asia, a female and male gibbon often pair up for many years. Every dawn and dusk they "duet" – sing and call to each other in turn. This helps the pair stay together to protect each other and raise their young.

Howler monkey
Alouetta (about 15 kinds)

HEIGHT	Head and body 60 cm, tail about the same
WEIGHT	Up to 10 kg
RANGE	Central and South America
DIET	Plant parts, mainly leaves, also fruits, buds, flowers, bark, some animal food such as eggs, grubs
HABITAT	Forests, woods
CONSERVATION STATUS	Some types are threatened

Like us, monkeys have forward-facing eyes. These allow them to judge distances accurately as they leap among branches.

The howler's throat is large with loose skin. It can blow up like a balloon when calling.

Inside the neck near the voicebox is a bone called the hyoid. We have this too, but the howler's hyoid is very large and helps to amplify, or make louder, the calls.

Howlers have a grasping or prehensile tail. This works as an extra arm-and-hand when climbing and swinging through the treetops.

STAY AWAY!

At dawn and dusk, if it is still and quiet, howlers can be heard 10 kilometres away, perhaps even further. Mainly the males call, telling other howler groups: "This is my territory, stay away!" Some of the sounds are to do with mating: "That's my female, clear off!"

LONELIEST LIFE

DEVIL'S HOLE PUPFISH

Devil's Hole pupfish live in a small pool below the desert in south-west North America – and nowhere else on Earth. They have adapted to the special conditions of warm water and food over the past 20,000 years.

In most years there are 400-500 pupfish at the end of summer. Some die in the winter, leaving only 100-200 pupfish to breed next spring.

Pupfish feed on tiny living things called diatoms, which are like micro-plants, plus other small food particles that fall or drift into the water.

MORE TINY HOMES

Various creatures have a very restricted range – they live in just one small area.

☆ The vaquita (below) is a small porpoise found only at the northern end of the Gulf of California, south-west North America. It is suited to the shallow, cloudy water and food sources here. Only 200-300 remain.

☆ Gilbert's potoroo is the most restricted marsupial (pouched mammal). It looks like a rabbit-sized shrew and survives on Bald Island and a tiny area of nearby mainland in south-west Australia.
Probably fewer than 50 are left.

DEATH VALLEY

Devil's Hole is near Death Valley, USA. In past years, people wanted to pump water from underground, for crops and new houses in the area. But the pumping lowered the pupfish's pool level and threatened them so it was stopped. The whole area is now protected by law.

The water in the pool is very warm, 33 degrees Celsius. Pupfish soon die if they are put in cooler water.

The pupfish are very small, only about 20 millimetres long, and blue in colour with silvery, black-edged fins.

Devil's Hole pupfish
Cyprinodon diabolis

LENGTH	20 mm
RANGE	The pool in Devil's Hole, south-west North America
DIET	Tiny plants and animals
HABITAT	Warm water in the pool
CONSERVATION STATUS	Vulnerable

THE SMALLEST HOME

★ Devil's Hole is a series of caves and passages in the Amaragosa Desert, Nevada, USA. The pupfish live in one pool here.

★ Water seeps into the pool from below. There are no streams or rivers to swim elsewhere.

★ The pool is very deep but the pupfish stay in the topmost few metres and rarely go down more than 20 metres.

BIGGEST SHOW-OFF

RAGGIANA BIRD-OF-PARADISE

Some of the most amazing sights in the animal world are birds-of-paradise. They flap wings, bob heads, shake their incredibly long bright-coloured feathers, dance and sing loudly. Why?

It's all to do with breeding. Only the male birds-of-paradise are so bright and colourful, and put on such a show. They want to attract females as mates.

PEACOCK PARADE

The male peacock has the largest tail in the bird world. To impress a peahen he lifts and spreads out the huge feathers with their eye-like pattern, and rattles them while crowing loudly. Can she fail to be impressed?

SHOWTIME

Why do male birds-of-paradise grow such astonishing plumage, and put on such fantastic displays? They hope to attract one of the females. If they do, the two mate. Then the female, who is a plain dull brown, goes off to nest and raise chicks alone.

The male shows off his amazing plumage by spreading his wings and then flapping them together as he bobs and shakes his head, jumps about, hangs upside down, flicks his tail over his head and much more!

FABULOUS FEATHERS

★ The male lyrebird of Australia has two wide striped tail plumes and many thin wispy ones. He holds them up in the shape of a musical instrument called a lyre.

★ The male quetzal from Central America has two gorgeous tail plumes known as streamers, which can be more than 60 centimetres in length.

Two long, thin, black tail feathers called "wires" trail out behind.

Bird-of-paradise
Paradisaea raggiana

LENGTH	Head-body 30-35 cm, male plumes 40-50 cm
WINGSPAN	50-60 cm
WEIGHT	Male 320 g, female 200 g
RANGE	New Guinea in South East Asia
DIET	Plant foods such as fruits, seeds and berries, small animals like bugs, frogs
HABITAT	Forests
CONSERVATION STATUS	No special status

Long feathers grow from the chest and form a reddish and chestnut-brown "cloak" around the bird.

The male Raggiana bird-of-paradise has a blue bill, yellow head, green chin, yellow collar and black chest.

103

SMELLIEST ANIMAL

ZORILLA

Several creatures might claim the prize of smelliest animal. One is the zorilla, also known as the striped polecat.

This African predator can frighten away lions, leopards and hyaenas simply by threatening to use its vile-smelling spray!

The zorilla is a cousin of weasels and stoats, with a similar shape of long, slim, bendy body and tail, and short legs.

BACK OFF OR I'LL SPRAY!

If the zorilla is threatened, it warns the enemy by arching its back and raising its tail. If this doesn't work, the zorilla whirls around and sprays the nasty fluid from its tail base. The choking smell makes creatures' eyes red, sore and watery, and hangs around for days.

The spray comes from anal glands under the tail and can be squirted out for a metre or more, along with stinking puffs of gas!

The vivid white and dark stripes are warning colours, like the skunk's. Other animals soon learn to link them with the terrible reek and so leave the zorilla alone.

SKUNK STINK AND DEVIL STENCH

☆ Another famously smelly animal is the skunk of North America. It has a defence display and horrible spray similar to the zorilla's.

☆ The Tasmanian devil (below) is an Australian marsupial (pouched mammal) that resembles a small dog. It's said to smell of rotting, decaying meat and putrid droppings.

Zorillas have sharp teeth and feed on all kinds of small creatures, as well as scavenging meat from carcasses (dead bodies).

PLAYING DEAD

If the zorilla's terrible smell does not work, it has more survival tricks. It may suddenly race to the nearest tree and scramble into the branches, being an excellent climber. Or it might simply play dead, lying still with foul fluids coming from its mouth, nose and rear end. Ugh!

Zorilla
Ictonyx striatus

LENGTH	Head-body 30 cm, tail 25 cm.
WEIGHT	1-1.4 kg
RANGE	Africa
DIET	Animals such as mice, rats, lizards, birds
HABITAT	Most habitats from forests to deserts
CONSERVATION STATUS	No special status

MOST UPSIDE DOWN

HOFFMAN'S TWO-TOED SLOTH

To us, the sloth's world looks topsy turvy. But to the sloth itself, upside down is right way up. This tropical tree-dweller spends more of its life hanging around than almost any other creature.

Sloths are truly slow. They may move only a few metres all day. But they don't need to. In their tropical forest home, they are surrounded by their food - there are leaves everywhere.

SLOTH + MOTH

Sloth fur teems with living things - beetles, lice, ticks, and even moths. Once each week the sloth goes down to the ground to leave droppings. The sloth moth lays its eggs in these, and the hatched caterpillars eat the dung.

SLOW AND SLEEPY

★ A sloth's body processes and chemistry, called its metabolism, are about half as fast as in other mammals.

★ This is because its leafy food provides little energy, so sloths have adapted to a slow lifestyle.

★ As part of this, sloths sleep a lot, between 10 and 12 hours on some days but up to 18 hours on others.

★ Also to save energy, a sloth does not bother to keep itself especially warm. Its body temperature may be only 30 degrees Celsius, compared to most mammals at 36-40 degrees.

★ So the sloth is the original hang-around-and-chill-out creature!

SWIFT-SWIMMING SLOTH

One activity that sloths do quite fast is swim. If their forest is flooded, they easily swim from one tree to the next. They "pull" with their front legs and "kick" with the back ones.

The feet and toes have specialized muscles and joints, so the sloth can hang'n'chill with almost no effort.

The claws are big, curved and sharp, to grip tree trunks and branches. They are also fierce weapons to slash and rip enemies.

Leaves are tricky to digest and contain little nourishment, so the belly is huge. In a well-fed sloth, two-thirds of the body weight is bulging stomach and guts!

The sloth's fur grows "upside down". Instead of the hairs sloping from body to feet, they lie the other way, for the rain to run down and off.

A sloth's head looks too small for its body, with little ears, big eyes and a flat snout.

Plant-like microbes on the hairs make them look mossy green, for better camouflage.

The neck is long, twisty and bendy, so the sloth can turn its head to look almost directly behind itself.

Hoffman's two-toed sloth

Choloepus hoffmanni

LENGTH	Head and body 50-70 cm, tail 3 cm
WEIGHT	5-8 kg
RANGE	Central America, Western South America
DIET	Leaves, also some flowers, fruits and buds
HABITAT	Tropical forests
CLAWS	Up to 7 cm long
CONSERVATION STATUS	No special status

SMALLEST BIRD'S NEST

The vervain hummingbird is speckled sparkly green on its back and wings, with a pale chin and chest. It's nowhere near as colourful as other small hummers.

VERVAIN HUMMINGBIRD

The smallest birds' nests belong to the smallest birds – hummingbirds. The very tiniest is built by the vervain hummingbird, which is itself the world's second-smallest bird, after its close cousin the bee hummingbird (page 34).

The nest is only needed for about six weeks, by which time the chicks have hatched, been fed, grown proper feathers - and flown away.

MEGA-NESTS

☆ **Largest single nest:** bald eagle (right). This stick-and-twig monster, called an eyrie, may be 3 metres wide, 6 metres deep and weigh over 2 tonnes!

☆ **Biggest communal (shared) nest:** sociable weaver bird. It reaches 6 metres wide and 3 metres tall, with more than 100 chambers, each for one pair of birds.

☆ **Most massive of all:** Australian mallee fowl. This "nest" is really a giant compost heap to keep the eggs inside warm. It may be 10 metres across, 4 metres high and 100 tonnes in weight.

LAZY MALE

The female vervain hummingbird chooses a male, the two mate ... and he clears off! She builds the nest and looks after her two eggs. And when the chicks hatch, she feeds and cares from them too.

The female makes her nest hidden in a bush, shrub or low tree, usually no more than one metre from the ground.

Vervain hummingbird
Mellisuga minima

LENGTH	6 cm
WEIGHT	2 G
RANGE	Caribbean Islands
DIET	Nectar, small bugs
HABITAT	Forests, parks, gardens
CONSERVATION STATUS	No special status

The nest is constructed from spider cobwebs and other spider silk, animal fur, soft feathers, and bendy plant parts such as spongy moss leaves and smooth cotton fibres.

CHAMPION NESTERS

☆ Some types of quail and partridge lay more than 20 eggs at one time, known as a clutch. And they may lay two or three clutches each spring-summer, making over 50 eggs each year.

☆ Most types of albatross lay only one egg at a time. The chick takes so long to grow up that the female produces one egg every two years.

☆ The eggs of small birds like finches and sparrows hatch after 11-12 days.

☆ An emperor penguin's egg hatches after 9 weeks of being balanced on the male's feet, to keep warm in the frozen Antarctic. No nesting materials there!

☆ A brown kiwi's egg takes as long as 11 weeks to hatch.

The cup-shaped nest is less than two centimetres across. Next time you see a walnut, look at the shell – the nest is almost half this size!

SNAPPIEST SPIDER

BRAZILIAN WANDERING SPIDER

In general, the biggest spiders – like tarantulas – do not have the most deadly bite. The strongest spider venom belongs to much smaller types like redbacks and black widows.

However, the Brazilian wandering spider is an exception. This big, strong creature would easily fill your hand. But never touch – it bites with lightning speed.

WHY SO DANGEROUS?

Wandering spiders (also known as huntsman spiders) are so deadly because:

☆ They have very strong venom, more than twice as powerful as a black widow's.

☆ They wander widely and do not seem worried about coming into gardens, sheds, huts and houses, or even cars and buses, where human contact is more likely.

☆ They like to spend the day somewhere dark and quiet, so they curl up in boxes, drawers, beds, even shoes and gloves!

MORE LETHAL SPIDERS

☆ The female black widow spider (right) is only small, but she can bite deeply for a long time. She's a "widow" because she may eat her male partner after mating.

☆ Australian funnelweb spiders are big and fierce, and bite hard in self-defence. Some kinds like to build homes in cellars and under sheds, making a human encounter more likely.

 FEARSOME FANGS

A spider bites by stabbing with its two fangs and pushing them together like pincers. Venom from a gland at the base of each fang pumps into the victim, to paralyze or even kill it. Then digestive juices dissolve the prey's flesh for the spider to suck in.

Brazilian wandering spider

Phoneutria (several species)

LENGTH	15 cm including legs
BODY	4 cm
WEIGHT	15-30 g
RANGE	Tropical South America
DIET	Animals, especially large insects such as crickets, also mice, lizards, frogs
HABITAT	Forests, swamps, farmlands, villages
CONSERVATION STATUS	No special status

When threatened, the spider raises its body, holds its front four legs up, and displays its reddish fangs, held ready to strike. Be warned or be bitten!

The spider sees with two big and six small eyes. It is also incredibly sensitive to touch and vibrations, which are more use in the darkness.

The wandering spider has long, strong, spiny legs, ideal for prowling among leaves, twigs and rocks at night.

Spider fangs, called chelicerae, are hard, curved, tooth-like parts, one on either side of the mouth. Each has a muscle-packed base that can move and tilt the fang itself.

The "wandering" spider is named because it searches the forest floor at night for prey, rather than weaving a web or waiting in a burrow.

MOST SINISTER SEASHELL

GEOGRAPHER'S CONE

"What a pretty seashell! Let's pick it up ... Ouch! It's given me a little sting. Never mind ... Arrgh!" That's a fatal mistake: never trust the lovely-looking but very venomous coneshell.

Coneshells are seasnails that slime along coasts and shallows, looking attractive and innocent. But they have a sinister secret. They can fire a deadly "spear" to kill their prey of small fish – or to repel an enemy.

ROCKPOOL DANGER

As well as coneshells, other venomous creatures lurk in rockpools along the shore.

☆ Auger shells, or terebras, stab and inject venom in a similar way to the coneshell.

☆ Killer fish include the stonefish (page 90) and the lacy-finned, long-spined lionfish or dragonfish.

☆ The blue-ringed octopus (left) has a body only the size of a tennis ball. But if its blue ring-like markings glow brighter, the octopus is ready to bite – and the venom can kills person.

Above the brown mottled crawling foot, the deadly "spear" is a tooth from the snail's radula (tongue) gripped by the end of the long, bendy proboscis.

DEADLY EFFECTS

There are hundreds of different types of coneshells. The geographer's cone has the strongest venom – and also the most attractive shell. This encourages people to pick it up ... More than 30 people are known to have died in this way.

Geographer's cone
Conus geographus

LENGTH	Up to 15 cm
CRAWLING HEIGHT	7-9 cm
RANGE	Indian and West Pacific Oceans
DIET	Small fish, prawns and similar sea creatures
HABITAT	Shores, reefs, shallow seas
CONSERVATION STATUS	No special status

Coneshells have barrel-like shells, flatter at one end and more tapered at the other, with a lengthways opening where the body sticks out.

The shiny, gorgeous shells of these seasnails mean that coneshells of all kinds are in danger from shell collectors.

The shell is beautifully marked with mottled patches and net-like lines, in shades of pale cream, light brown, chestnut-brown, violet and purple.

LETHAL WEAPON

The coneshell's proboscis extends like a tiny elephant's trunk and thrusts in the "spear", which is hollow, see-through and made of hard minerals. Venom pumps through the hollow spear which, like a harpoon on its cord, is attached to the coneshell by a stringy thread. As the victim becomes paralyzed the coneshell pulls it near for swallowing.

HOTTEST HOME

GIANT DEEP-SEA TUBEWORM

Deep in the world's oceans it is totally black, almost freezing, and crushingly high-pressured, for thousands of kilometres all around.

But here and there on the sea floor, jets of superhot water squirt out from cracks and holes. All kinds of weird life-forms thrive around these deep-sea hydrothermal vents.

SMOKING CHIMNEYS

As superhot vent water emerges, it cools in seconds. Dissolved minerals in it turn into tiny particles that form smoke-like clouds, usually black or white, which drift away in the darkness. Other minerals go hard and gradually build up tall tubes and chimney-like towers around the vent, some more than 50 metres high.

The worm's feathery red "plume" is the part that both takes in oxygen to breathe, and takes in minerals as food.

Deep-sea vents are like geysers on land. Water superheated to more than 400 degrees Celsius, by the magma (melted rocks) deep below, shoots out of gaps into the cold water around, which is just 2 degrees.

VENT VILLAGE

Strange, little-known animals live around hydrothermal vents. Many are blind because there is no light here.

☆ The vent crab is ghostly white and grows to about 12 cm across.

☆ Fish known as deep-sea eelpouts cruise around, looking for small shrimps and seasnails.

☆ Vent mussels 20 cm long filter water for food and also have helpful bacteria inside, like tubeworms.

☆ Other vent creatures include squat lobsters, clams, shrimps and dandelion-jellyfish.

Around the vent are giant deep-sea tubeworms, taller than a human and as thick as your arm.

The tube is made of the hard substance chitin, like an insect's body casing. The worm can withdraw into in for safety.

SULPHUR FEASTS

Giant tubeworms have no mouth or guts. But they do contain millions of microbes called bacteria. The worm's red plume takes in minerals such as sulphides from the water. The bacteria break down the minerals to produce energy and food, which they share with the worm.

Other creatures crowd around the vent – crabs, worms, shellfish, and fish like this vent eelpout. They form a busy little community of life, in contrast to the near-emptiness around.

Giant deep-sea tubeworm

Riftia pachyptila

LENGTH	Up to 2.5 m
WEIGHT	5 kg or more
RANGE	Deep sea, usually below 1,000 m
DIET	Food made by microbes inside them, from minerals in the water
HABITAT	Hydrothermal vents
CONSERVATION STATUS	No special status

STRONGEST INSECT

AUSTRALIAN HORNED DUNG BEETLE

Mighty insects put tug-of-warring and weightlifting humans in the shade! These six-legged powerhouses can push, pull, roll or lift hundreds of times their own body weight, easily beating people.

Such feats are possible because of body size. As these creatures become larger, their muscles, skeletons, guts and other parts become heavier very quickly, so the overall strength-to-weight comparison falls fast.

FEATS OF STRENGTH

★ **Pull-push** Scientific tests showed that the Australian horned dung beetle can shift 1,141 times its own weight. That's the same as a person towing over 10 fully loaded school buses.

★ **Lift** The rhinoceros beetle can hoist aloft more than 800 times its body weight. To match that, a human would have to pick up a fully-loaded, battle-ready army tank.

★ **Carry** Leafcutter ants cart objects weighing 100 times more than themselves, for many metres. If human, they would carry a family car more than 2 km!

The beetle uses its mouthparts and legs to slice out and shape a chunk of moist dung into an easily-rolled ball shape.

Almost standing on its head, the beetle pushes the ball with its rear four legs while gripping the ground with its front pair.

Australian horned dung beetle

Onthophagus taurus

LENGTH	2–3 cm
RANGE	Australia
DIET	Dung
HABITAT	Grasslands, shrub, open woodland
CONSERVATION STATUS	No special status

(S) MIGHTY MITE

Mites are eight-legged relatives of spiders, and can be even stronger than insects. The tropical moss mite that easily fits in this "o" can withstand a pull of almost 1,200 times its own weight.

Dung beetles love fresh animal droppings or dung, especially from large plant-eaters such as cattle, horses, zebras, antelopes, gazelles and deer.

The beetle digs a hole for the ball, lays her eggs on the dung and covers it with earth. When the grubs hatch, the dung is their delicious food!

(S) STRONG-ARM OF THE JUNGLE

Gorillas, along with chimps, are our close animal cousins. But the male gorilla far out-muscles any person. Tests show that its upper body strength, in the arms, shoulders and chest, can be five times greater than a human's.

FREAKIEST FISH

Deep-sea anglerfish

Melanocetus johnsoni

LENGTH	10-15 cm
RANGE	Worldwide
DIET	Other creatures
HABITAT	Deep sea, usually below 100 m
CONSERVATION STATUS	No special status

DEEP-SEA ANGLERFISH

It's a weird world in the dark depths of the ocean. Some of the most extraordinary sights are deep-sea anglerfish – or rather, all you see is their "bait".

These freaky-looking creatures fish for food with light as the lure. There are several kinds of anglerfish and their close relations, goosefish and frogfish.

 MAKING LIGHT

☆ The ability of living things to make light is called bioluminescence.

☆ Nine-tenths of all deep-sea creatures do this, from jellyfish (right, above) to the weird gulper eel (right, below).

☆ The light comes from a chemical reaction involving two substances, luciferin and luciferase.

☆ This may happen inside the animal's own body cells, or in friendly bacteria living in its body.

A REAL BIG-MOUTH

Food is scarce in the vast dimness of the deep ocean. So the bigger your mouth, the more chance you have of catching something. Gulper eels and pelican eels take this to the extreme, with a massive mouth and tiny tail-like body.

No light means no one can see colours or patterns, so the anglerfish is drab brown or grey.

At the spine's end is a fleshy lump that can glow in the dark. Curious fish and other small creatures come near to investigate.

A long, rod-like fin spine extends from the nose. Usually this arches up and over, down to the fish's mouth. Muscles at the spine base move and wave it to waggle the bait.

The body is rounded with small fins. At great depth there's no need for streamlined speed. To escape danger, the anglerfish turns off its light lure and slides away into the blackness.

FLASHING LIGHTS

☆ Lanternfish have rows of light spots along the body, so they can recognize each other when looking for mates in the darkness.

☆ One type of lanternfish, called the flashlightfish, can turn its 'headlights' on and off! It has a large glow-spot near each eye, and a flap to pull over it to stop the light.

... GULP! The anglerfish opens its massive mouth and swallows the prey whole in one great "suck".

BEST SHOT

ARCHERFISH

The award for champion animal sharpshooter goes to a little striped fish! Known as the archerfish, it uses its tongue and mouth as a water pistol to squirt "arrows of water" at its food.

One moment an insect is resting peacefully on a leaf or twig just above the surface. Next second – splash, the jet of water hits. Then – plop, in it falls, to be gobbled up by the archerfish.

 ## ANGLING SPIDER

The bolas spider or fishing spider (below) twirls around a strand of its silk thread, which has a sticky blob or "bolas" at the end. The blob sticks to a fly, moth or similar passing creature, and the spider pulls it in, like an angler reeling in a fish on a hook-and-line..

4. FIRE! The fish pokes its snout above the surface, squeezes its gills fast and squirts a fierce jet of water through its tongue-tunnel, to knock the target off its perch into the water.

ARCHER'S EYESIGHT

Archerfish can swivel their eyes to see their prey better and judge distance. Also, because light rays bend as they enter water, the archer learns to aim slightly lower, higher, or to the side, compared to where it sees the prey, according to the prey's distance and angle.

3. TAKE AIM The fish spots a victim above the water. Using specially adapted eyes, it adjusts its body position and angle, ready to shoot.

2. READY It makes a U shape with its strong, bendy tongue, and presses this against the roof of its mouth to form a tube.

Archerfish
Toxotes (several species)

LENGTH	Usually 20-25 cm, up to 40 cm
WEIGHT	Up to 700 g
RANGE	South, East and South East Asia, Australia, West Pacific
DIET	Small creatures, also seeds, fruits, other plant parts
HABITAT	Rivers, swamps, estuaries, coastal waters
JET RANGE	Up to 5 m, but accurate usually at 1-2 m
CONSERVATION STATUS	No special status

1. LOCK'N'LOAD The archer takes in a large mouthful of water, allowing its gills and gill covers to bend outwards.

The fish's body has upright stripes for camouflage, to hide among water plants and tree roots.

MOST RECENT MAJOR EXTINCTION

BAIJI

When a living thing becomes extinct, it means that all of its kind have died out – gone forever. Only a few years ago this was the tragic fate of the shy, secretive, peaceful baiji (Chinese or Yangtze river dolphin).

This amazing creature was killed off by chemical and waste pollution, people catching its fishy food, being caught itself as food, getting tangled and drowned in nets, suffering hits from boats and catching diseases.

 ON THE EDGE

Hundreds of other large animal species stare extinction in the face:

☆ Island fox (below) – a few hundred left on the Channel Islands, California, USA
☆ Florida bonneted bat – hardly ever seen nowadays in the south of this US state.
☆ Javan rhino – probably fewer than 50 survive.

The blowhole on the head was the breathing opening, and closed when the dolphin dived under the surface.

COUNTDOWN TO OBLIVION

★ **Ancient times** 5,000 or more baijis
★ **1980s** Probably 200-300 left.
★ **2002** The last captive baiji died.
★ **2004** The last wild baiji was seen.
★ **2006** Scientists and wildlife experts searched along the Yangtze, but found none.
★ **2007** The baiji was declared "probably extinct".
★ **Since 2007** Nothing.

Muddy water means eyes are not much use, so they were small with poor vision.

The long, thin snout had about 60-70 fish-grabbing teeth in each of the upper and lower jaws.

Baiji
Lipotes vexillifer

LENGTH 2.5 m
WEIGHT 150-200 kg
RANGE Yangtze River (Cháng Jiang) in East China, lakes and rivers joined to it
DIET Fish and other water animals
HABITAT Fresh water of rivers, lakes, swamps
CONSERVATION STATUS Officially critically endangered, but probably extinct

GONE BEFORE WE KNOW

Extinctions probably happen many times each year. Most are small bugs in tropical forests cut down for timber, farms, houses, factories, mines and quarries. Scientists have not studied these forests, so we do not even know which creatures live there. But the chances are high that unique species are being lost for all time.

NEWEST SPECIES

CRAZY COLOURS

The "psychedelic" gecko (below) is an amazingly-coloured lizard first found in 2010 on an expedition to Hon Khoai Island, Vietnam, South East Asia. Islands are excellent places for unique species. Each island has its own distinctive conditions, to which creatures adapt by evolving, and so become new species.

FOJA MOUNTAINS FOREST WALLABY

Every year, wildlife experts find new kinds of creatures. Some are in remote, dangerous places, such as mountainous forests or the deep sea.

Others are already known, but we did not realize that what we thought was one kind of creature, is in fact two or more different species.

VEGGIE SPIDER

All spiders eat only prey creatures - except the vegetarian jumping spider (Bagheera kiplingi, below). It eats mainly the nutrient-packed, bud-like parts on the leaf tips of certain acacia trees. However it keeps up the great hunting tradition of spiders by catching small caterpillars and even snacking on young of its own kind.

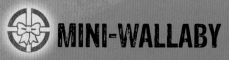
MINI-WALLABY

The tiniest member of the kangaroo family (below) was discovered in 2008 by an expedition to the Foja Mountains of New Guinea, South East Asia. It is a relative of two other kinds of known forest wallabies from the same region.

LOST AND FOUND

"Lazarus" animals are those thought to have died out long ago, but then rediscovered.

★ In 2011 the rainbow long-legged toad was sighted again in Borneo after a gap of nearly 90 years.

★ After more than 100 years, in 1999 the La Gomera giant lizard was found surviving on the island of La Gomera (part of the Canary Islands).

Foja Mountains forest wallaby

Dorcopsulus

HEIGHT	30 cm
LENGTH	60-80 cm
WEIGHT	3-5 kg
RANGE	Foja Mountains, New Guinea
DIET	Leaves, fruits, other plant parts
HABITAT	Tropical forest
CONSERVATION STATUS	Not decided yet

GLOSSARY

Amphibians
Animals with a backbone and usually four legs, that begin life in water as swimming tadpoles which breathe using gills. They grow up able to breathe with lungs and live on land. The main amphibian groups are frogs, toads, newts, salamanders, and worm-like caecilians.

Arthropods
Animals with a tough outer skeleton, like a body casing, which has legs that can bend at specialized joints. They include insects, spiders and other arachnids, crabs and other crustaceans, millipedes and centipedes.

Blowholes
The breathing openings of water-dwelling mammals – whales, dolphins and porpoises. They are on top of the head and connected to the passageways inside the nose, mouth and lungs.

Camouflage
Shapes, colours or patterns an animal displays to blend in with the surroundings and to hide from predators or prey.

Canine teeth
Long, pointed teeth at the front sides of the mouth. They are usually large and fang-like in predatory animals such as cats and wolves. They form long tusks in narwhals, walrus and some deer.

Carnivore
A creature that kills and eats other animals to obtain energy and nutrients, and does not regularly eat plants. Big cats such as lions, and polar bears are examples of carnivorous animals.

Chitin
A strong, tough substance made by certain animals. Chitin forms the outer body casing of insects, and parts of the shell in shellfish.

Cold-blooded
The popular name given to animals that do not make warmth inside their own bodies, but rely on heat sources like the sun to keep their bodies warm. The majority of living things, such as insects, spiders, crabs and fish, are cold-blooded.

Dorsal
On the back or upper side of an animal. For example, the fin on top of a fish, on its back, is the dorsal fin.

Echolocation
The use of sound to find the way and detect objects. The sounds are sent out by an animal, who then listens for any echoes that bounce back off nearby objects. The direction, strength and timing of the echoes shows what is nearby. This system is used by bats, some whales and dolphins, and a few shrews, birds and insects.

Extinction
The death of all members of a group of living things, so that they no longer exist. The group is usually a species, but it may be one variety or subspecies within a species, or even a whole collection of species.

Evolution
The tendency of all living things to change over time, as they adapt to or suit their surroundings. Evolution usually happens over thousands or millions of years.

Flukes
The wide, flap-like parts of a whale's tail, often shaped like a Y or T seen from above.

Habitat
A particular kind of living place or surroundings, such as a pond, river, mountain, pine forest, tropical forest, desert, grassland, lake, swamp, rocky seashore, muddy shore, coral reef or deep sea bed. The urban habitat is one where people live and includes buildings, roads, parks and gardens. Most kinds of animals are suited to one or a few habitats. Others, such as the red fox or brown rat, are adaptable and can survive in many habitats.

Hibernation
An extra-long, extra-deep sleep, usually during cold conditions. A warm-blooded animal slows down its breathing, heartbeat and other body processes, and allows its body temperature to fall to that of its surroundings.

Incisor teeth
Sharp teeth at the front of the mouth. They are especially chisel-like and always growing in rodent mammals such as rats and mice. Very long incisors form the tusks of elephants.

Mammals
Warm-blooded animals that have a backbone and skeleton, fur or hair, and feed their young on mother's milk. Even 'hairless' mammals like whales and rhinos have some small hairs, usually around the nose as whiskers.

Marine
A general term for anything connected with salty water, seas and oceans. It is used to describe the plants and animals that inhabit this area. Sharks and whales are marine creatures.

Migration
A long journey, usually made at the same time each year. Many animals undertake regular two-way migrations, there and back again, for reasons such as finding food and somewhere safe to breed.

Nectar
A sweet, sugary, high-energy fluid made by plants, especially certain flowers. It attracts animals such as bees, butterflies and other insects, birds and bats, who come to feed on it. In the process they carry the plant's pollen to other plants of the same kind, so these can form seeds.

Omnivore
A creature that eats both animal and plant foods to obtain energy and nutrients. Humans are omnivorous, and so are pigs, most bears and some lizards.

Parasite
A living thing that obtains food, shelter, warmth, protection or some other need from another living thing, known as the host, and in the process causes damage or harm to the host. Plants such as mistletoe and dodder, and animals like mosquitoes and tapeworms, are all parasites.

Plankton
Aquatic living things that float freely in open water, both in the seas and oceans, and in the fresh water of lakes and rivers. Most plankton cannot actively swim, rather they drift where currents take them. There are many different living things in most plankton, including tiny animals and plants, the young stages of larger creatures, microscopic bacteria and other living things.

Poison
A substance that causes harm when it is taken into a living thing, usually by being eaten, breathed in, or soaking in through the skin. Many kinds of living things make poisons, including microbes like bacteria, toadstools and other fungi, flowers such as deadly nightshade, and animals like pufferfish and certain frogs and toads.

Predator
A carnivorous (meat-eating) animal that survives by catching, killing and eating other animals. Wolves, tigers and sharks are all predators, and so are snakes and spiders.

Prehensile
Able to grip, grasp or hold. Some monkeys and lizards have a prehensile tail that can curl around and grasp objects.

Quills
Long structures that grow out of the skin of some animals. In mammals they are specialized thick, stiff, long hairs. Some quills, like those of porcupines, are sharply pointed and used for defence. Bird feathers have a stiff central shaft known as a quill.

Reptiles
The group of mostly four-legged, scaly-skinned animals with a backbone. It includes turtles, tortoises, terrapins, lizards, snakes, crocodiles and alligators. Most reptiles are cold-blooded.

Rodents
Mammals with long, sharp front teeth, called incisors, designed to gnaw, bite and nibble. These teeth keep growing through life. There are more than 2,200 kinds or species in the rodent group, including rats, mice, voles, hamsters, squirrels, gophers, chipmunks, prairie dogs, marmots, beavers, guinea-pigs and porcupines.

Scutes
Hard, bony, plate-like structures under or within the skin that form the protective coverings of animals such as turtles, crocodiles and armadillos.

Skeleton
A hard, strong framework or supporting part. Animals such as mammals, birds, reptiles, amphibians and fish have a bony skeleton on the inside. Insects and crabs have a skeleton on the outside, as a tough body casing.

Species
A particular kind or type of living thing. All members of a species look similar and can breed together, but they cannot usually breed with other species. Each species has a unique two-part scientific name. For example, all tigers belong to one species, Panthera tigris. However all elephants are not one species. There are three elephant species: African bush elephant, Loxodonta africana; African forest elephant, Loxodonta cyclotis; and Asian elephant, Elephas maximus.

Torpor
When cold-blooded creatures like frogs, snakes, fish and butterflies become inactive in cold conditions, they are said to be in a state of torpor. They cannot make heat in their bodies and their muscles do not work when cold.

Venom
A harmful substance made by an animal that is jabbed or stabbed into the victim from the outside, usually by special body parts such as fangs, spines or stingers.

Vertebrae
The collective name for the bones that form the backbone, spinal column or spine of the skeleton. Each of these bones individually is called a vertebra. Humans have 33 vertebrae, while long-bodied animals like snakes have more than 200. Invertebrate animals do not have vertebrae.

Warm-blooded
The popular name given to animals that make heat inside their bodies, by breaking down and "slow-burning" food energy, so the body temperature stays high and constant. The main warm-blooded groups are mammals and birds. A few insects and fish can also be warm-blooded under certain conditions.

Wingspan
The distance between the two wingtips of a winged animal such as a bird, bat or insect, when the wings are outstretched.

CREDITS

The publishers would like to thank the following sources for their kind permission to reproduce the pictures in this book. Every effort has been made to correctly acknowledge and contact the source and/or copyright holder of each picture, and Carlton Books Limited apologizes for any unintentional errors or omissions, which will be corrected in future editions of this book.

PICTURE CREDITS:

The publishers would like to thank the following sources for their kind permission to reproduce the pictures in this book. Key, T=top, L=left, R=right, B=bottom

Alamy: /Nic Hamilton: 86, /Stone Nature Photography: 100-101 © **Carlton Books** 64-65 **Corbis:** /Mark Moffett/Minden Pictures: 96br, /Norbert Wu/Minden Pictures: 120b, /NASA: 89, /National Geographic Society: 51, /Denis Scott: 10-11, 48-49, /Jack Milchanowski/Visuals Unlimited: 4b, 75 **FLPA:** 64, /Emanuele Biggi: 112-113, /Neil Bowman: 50-51, /Christian Handl/Imagebroker: 94, /Imagebroker: 7cr, /W T Miller: 104-105, /Carr Clifton/Minden Pictures: 80, /Mitsuhiko Imamori/Minden Pictures: 118-119, /Donald M. Jones/Minden Pictures: 80-81, /Scott Linstead/Minden Pictures: 74, /Thomas Marent/Minden Pictures: 72-73, /Hiroya Minakuchi/Minden Pictures: 68-69, /Mark Moffet/Minden Pictures: 106, /Flip Nicklin/Minden Pictures: 56-57, 57r, /Pete Oxford/Minden Pictures: 6l, 110-111, /Patricio Robles Gil/Minden Pictures: 54-55, /Kevin Schafer/Minden Pictures: 124, /Norbert Wu/Minden Pictures: 36-37, 68, 121 /Photo Researchers: 17, /Panda Photo: 86-87, /Harri Taavetti: 16, /D P Wilson: 71 **Getty Images:** 54, /Guillermo Armenteros, Dominican Republic: 108-109, /Mark Conlin: 24b, /Stephen Dalton: 7P 79, /Carol Farneti-Foster: 126, /Rick Gaffney: 20b, /Jeff Hunter: 88-89, /National Geographic: 19, /Nature Picture Library: 42b, /Alastair Pollock: 20-21, /Luis Javier Sandoval: 13 **iStockphoto.com:** 11c, 12-13, 35r, 59r **Naturepl.com:** /Martin Camm (WAC): 100, /Mark Carwardine: 124-125, /Georgette Douma: 114, /Jurgen Freund: 90, /Edwin Giesbers: 84-85, /Tim Laman: 127, /Rolf Nussbaumer: 108, /Doug Perrine: 19br, /Jeff Rotman: 114-115, /Phil Savoie: 102-103, /Kim Taylor: 122-123, /David Tipling: 98-99, /Dave Watts: 7r, **NHPA:** /A.N.T Photography: 122 **Press Association Images:** /Lee Grismer/AP: 126r **Rex Features:** 82-83 **Science Photo Library:** /Steve Gschmeissner: 110, /London School of Hygiene: 92, Dr Ken MacDonald: 116-117, /NOAA: 116, /Kenreth Bart/Visuals Unlimited: 62b **Steve Jones:** 66-67 **Thinkstockphotos.co.uk:** 2-3, 4tl, 4tr, 6t, 6r, 7tl, 7tr, 7bl, 7br, 8-9, 14-15, 18, 22-23, 24-25, 25t, 26-27, 28-29, 30-31, 32-33, 34-35, 37, 38-39, 40-41, 42-43, 44b, 46-47, 48, 50-51, 52-53, 53, 57t, 58-59, 60-61, 62-63, 66, 70-71, 73, 76-77, 78b, 79t, 83, 84, 90-91, 92-93, 94-95, 96br, 97, 98b, 102, 105, 106-107, 112, 119, 120c

Every effort has been made to acknowledge correctly and contact the source and/or copyright holder of each picture and Carlton Books Limited apologises for any unintentional errors or omissions, which will be corrected in future editions of this book.